T0291270

Knowledge Management for Project Excellence

Knowledge Management for Project Excellence defines a methodology, called Projects with Learning Outcomes (ProwLO), for management of knowledge in projects, including a process model. This guide enables organizations to solve many known knowledge management problems as experienced in practice.

The process model consists of eight processes, which are in turn made of activities. These processes are aligned with the generic life cycle of projects and programmes. They drive knowledge processes in project environments. ProwLO is a tool to institutionalize knowledge processing and optimize knowledge processes, and thereby provides the infrastructure for the development of learning organizations.

This book, as a methodology, provides a lot of contextual information for a better understanding of knowledge management in the context of projects. First of all, it provides an understanding of the essence of knowledge. Second, examples of knowledge needs are provided in the context of two PRINCE2 processes and risk management. Third, it provides extensive background information on project management.

This book offers a step-by-step guide to executing a successful project management in the context of the key processes. It also provides the reader with a decision-making tool, supported by the capture of Cases, a key experience knowledge type. As such, it is an essential tool for any project manager operating in the knowledge economy.

Lukasz Rosinski has a bachelor's degree in Information Sciences and a master's degree in Business Informatics from Utrecht University. He is the founder of KnowledgePlace, a document management system for project-based and project-driven organizations. He is also co-founder of CyberKnowmad, a knowledge sharing platform.

Knowledge Management for Project Excellence

Lukasz Rosinski

Routledge
Taylor & Francis Group

LONDON AND NEW YORK

First published 2020
by Routledge
2 Park Square, Milton Park, Abingdon, Oxon OX14 4RN

and by Routledge
52 Vanderbilt Avenue, New York, NY 10017

Routledge is an imprint of the Taylor & Francis Group, an informa business

British Library Cataloguing-in-Publication Data
A catalogue record for this book is available from the British Library

Library of Congress Cataloging-in-Publication Data
Names: Rosinski, Lukasz, author.
Title: Knowledge management for project excellence / Lukasz Rosinski.
Description: 1. Edition. | New York : Routledge, 2019. |
Includes bibliographical references and index.
Identifiers: LCCN 2019027631 | ISBN 9780367351144 (hardback) |
ISBN 9780429329975 (ebook)
Subjects: LCSH: Knowledge management. | Project management.
Classification: LCC HD30.2 .R6636 2019 | DDC 658.4/038–dc23
LC record available at https://lccn.loc.gov/2019027631

ISBN: 978-0-367-35114-4 (hbk)
ISBN: 978-0-429-32997-5 (ebk)

Typeset in Baskerville
by Integra Software Services Pvt. Ltd.

MIX
Paper from
responsible sources
FSC
www.fsc.org   FSC™ C013985

Printed in the United Kingdom
by Henry Ling Limited

Contents

Figures

Tables

Acknowledgements

The author thanks Sjaak Brinkkemper for teaching process-data modelling, introducing the concept of meta-models, and his role in developing the EFD technique.

Remko Helms, for his introduction to KM and for sharing key insights, such as, for example, the lack of consensus on the distinction between knowledge and information, that knowledge processes apply to all conceptual knowledge needs (based on a uniform life cycle) and are differentiated based on the roles involved, and the impracticality of particular approaches to knowledge classification.

Jan Herman Verpoorten, for his introduction to PRINCE2, and his key insight that PRINCE2 is above all a process model, a better description than a 'collection of best practices'.

Academic work in general that contributed to my general domain knowledge of both KM and PM, and the rare but gold papers on the frontier of both.

Research opportunities at corporations for testing and validating my knowledge.

In the process of writing this book I received much feedback from various subject experts. Thanks to their role, providing insightful input, many improvements were carried out on various levels. To mention a few people, Adrian Dooley for rethinking strategic alignment with other P3M frameworks, stressing the importance of compatibility with alternative approaches. Stanisław Gasik for extensive feedback on this book proposal early in the process, posing fundamental questions and querying statements lacking clarification.

Introduction

Project knowledge management (PKM) is a process that is concerned with managing knowledge that relates to or arises from projects. Thanks to formal project management approaches, projects generate a lot of information used within the project's scope and beyond. This information is vital for successfully managing the project. Specific knowledge that arises from the project can also be used to improve future project processes and increase the chance of project success. Knowledge reuse is a major driver for PKM.

For a better understanding of PKM, the following definition of knowledge management (KM) is adopted:

> a management discipline that seeks to have impact on knowledge processing.
>
> (McElroy, 2003)

Knowledge management and knowledge processing are constantly confused. KM is concerned with strategy and planning KM initiatives in alignment with the business strategy of an organization. Knowledge processing, on the other hand, is at the operational level and covers the life cycle of knowledge or codified knowledge objects.

A standardized approach, such as ProwLO (**Pro**jects **w**ith **L**earning **O**utcomes), is developed to institutionalize knowledge processing in a project-driven or project-dependent environment. In the case of project-driven organizations, the primary business is made up of projects. Examples include engineering companies, such as general contractors and software development firms that develop tailor-made solutions. In the case of project-dependent organizations, projects are not the core business and are usually sponsored and funded internally. Examples include manufacturing (consumer goods, engineered products), banking and financial services, and pharmaceuticals. ProwLO is all about knowledge reuse across projects. So in case of project-driven organizations, it is essential. In case of project-dependent organizations, it is highly beneficial as project knowledge may have generic value. Both classes of organization, introduced by Russel Archibald (2004), are examples of 'project-based organizations', an umbrella concept for environments characterized by projects.

In order to better understand knowledge processing in project environments it is essential to elaborate on project knowledge as a concept. In the literature, a distinction is often made between **explicit** and **tacit** knowledge. Explicit knowledge is the type of knowledge that can be articulated, codified and communicated in symbolic form and/or natural language. Tacit knowledge is the type of knowledge that is much harder to communicate and formalize as it is deeply rooted in action, commitment and involvement in a specific context. Most scholars agree that through modes of knowledge conversion, introduced by Nonaka (1994), tacit knowledge can be converted into explicit knowledge, and vice versa. These modes are: Socialization (tacit-to-tacit); Combination (explicit-to-explicit); Externalization (tacit-to-explicit); and Internalization (explicit-to-tacit). According to Nonaka's theory, organizational knowledge enters different states and transformations, starting with the individual and then growing into existence in larger groups. These dynamics are described as a continuous dialogue or interplay between tacit and explicit knowledge involving the different modes of conversion, and depicted as a growing spiral flow as knowledge moves through individual, group and organizational levels. For example, according to Nonaka, the use of metaphors, a common expression, is a perfect example of externalizing tacit knowledge. Cook and Brown (1999), on the other hand, argue that conversion of knowledge is not possible; they believe that explicit and tacit knowledge are generated and disseminated each in its own right. In their understanding, the source of new knowledge and knowing lies in the use of knowledge as a tool of knowing within situated interaction with the social and physical world (Cook & Brown, 1999, p. 383). This is called the generative dance. So there is a distinction between knowledge *used* in action and knowing *as part of action*. By comparing these two theories, a philosophical discussion may follow, but from a practical point of view, the point of ProwLO, the notion of externalization is critical as codified knowledge is easier to disseminate and is not affected by amnesia (unless forgotten in archives or confronted with data loss). Whether the externalized knowledge accurately resembles the original tacit knowledge, justifying the claim of knowledge conversion, is interesting but not the main concern. Most important is that, in any case, the process of externalization can be regarded as knowledge production and that explicit knowledge can be used as a tool of knowing anyway. As noted online (Larsen & Eargle, 2015), without explicit knowledge, tacit knowledge conversion becomes a closed loop. Internalization, on the other hand, simply corresponds to the traditional notion of learning. There is no real point in discussing the nature of internalized explicit knowledge from a KM perspective. From a learning perspective, it leans towards cognitive science, which is not the focus of this book. For the reader, it suffices to know that internalized explicit knowledge contributes to the development of mental modes and potentially challenges the existing ways of doing. Based on Huber's (1991) observation of organizations, one can infer that an individual learns if his or her range of 'potential' behaviour and/or thinking processes is changed.

It *is*, however, possible to unite the two opposite models by means of a continuum of knowledge conversion effectiveness, with perfect knowledge, on the one end, and conversion and fragmented, on the other. The key proposition here is that if Nonaka's model results in imperfect knowledge conversion, then Cooke and Browns model complements by additional 'knowing' in which the user engages with the knowledge in question, for example, by knowledge application. The effectiveness of knowledge conversion in a social context (which often sets the stage) is arguably a function of the skills and specialized techniques involved, complexity and related fragmentation, and shared understanding (influenced by cognitive ability).

More often debated by scholars is the distinction between knowledge and information. In the context of ProwLO, a definition of knowledge is not adopted. Instead, ProwLO makes a distinction between project management (PM) information and reusable project knowledge. The former is the type of information that is limited to the scope of single projects, albeit based on needs of senior management, programme directors, the Project Board, project team members, etc. The latter is the type of information that has greater generic value. It does not mean that reusable project knowledge can be completely detached from projects it was derived. In the event of knowledge reuse, it may be necessary to consider the project context as well. It should be stressed that not all project knowledge has roots in a similar past project. It could be acquired externally.

PM information is closely tied to the adopted PM approach, such as, for example, PRINCE2. ProwLO is developed to work with but is not limited to PRINCE2. The reason is that projects using PRINCE2 produce a lot of management information. All PRINCE2 management products contain such information. Some regard this as cumbersome but they forget that PRINCE2 can be tailored and scaled to the specific needs of a particular project. In any case, it can be asserted that PRINCE2 greatly satisfies the knowledge needs of the Project Board and other members of the PM team based on the extensive scope of this method. Another key argument for choosing PRINCE2 is that some PRINCE2 activities lead to reusable project knowledge, most notably the support for the capture of Lessons Learned.

Reusable project knowledge is closely tied to a knowledge life cycle. Managing such project knowledge is a continuous process that transcends the time and space boundaries of single projects (Chen et al., 2003). ProwLO defines a Project Knowledge Value Chain that captures knowledge processes as part of this life cycle (see Chapter 3, section 'Define and Plan Knowledge Activities'). Some processes occur within projects, and some do not. Accordingly, PKM can be viewed at two levels: organization and project. At the project level, ProwLO establishes PKM as a component of projects, a sub-function. It is not a component of PM by most common definitions. This postulation is supported by the lack of reference in PM guides and handbooks – there are exceptions, like the PRINCE2 manual which shows overlap in areas such as Lessons Learned. Second, by the current lack of knowledge management practice in project environments. A root cause for the latter is that a defined approach for something as complex was lacking until now. On the other hand, without adopting a well-written and exclusive definition of PM, the status of PKM remains open to debate. It is arguably a philosophical discussion anyway. For example, if we consider the parallel of managing product delivery, also a sub-function of projects (see Figure 4 for an overall depiction), it is difficult not to associate it with PM, especially in the world of Agile. While managing product delivery is the responsibility of the Team Manger role, the main actor in PKM is the Project Knowledge Manager, essential to ProwLO. Organizational promotion of PKM as a distinct function and acknowledgement of a Project Knowledge Manager as a support role in projects are two key success factors. That said, there is a natural tension between PM and PKM at the project level because PM is goal-oriented and deals with time pressure, whereas PKM is not an end in itself and has a long-term focus.

ProwLO's aim is two-fold. First, to satisfy the knowledge needs of project members in *high-level* PRINCE2 projects *or* any type of endeavour with similar project/programme life cycle management (e.g. the Praxis Framework), but different detailed processes. So, knowledge reuse is not an end in itself, there has to be a valid link with specific knowledge needs. In relation to high-level PRINCE2, PINO (PRINCE2 in name only) is not a bad thing when the organization has a tailored methodology supporting effective PM. PM can be effective across the organization repeatedly only if well defined and managed as a key capability, characteristic for mature organizations. Ideally, any specific methodology should support optimization of *organizational* capability and be flexible enough to incorporate ProwLO to facilitate such business improvement. Optimization is generally associated with maximal maturity levels in specific areas based on assessment method. The level of commitment to optimization and tolerance to necessary change is a perfect indicator whether an organization classifies as 'learning organization'. Empirical evidence derived from maturity assessments shows that there is a long way to go for most organizations to attain such status. Arguably, a more holistic approach than process management, a discipline often practised, is required to advance an organization to the highest levels of maturity, for sustainable capability (not to be confused with competitive advantage) and greater proficiency. Similar to knowledge reuse, organizational maturity is not an end in itself. In relation to suitability for programmes, as a distinct undertaking from a project, the Praxis Framework shows that both types of endeavours are very similar in terms of life cycle characteristics. The main difference is that the degree of complexity in programmes is affected by less integrated delivery of programme elements as part of a broader defined scope (relatively bigger as compared to a conventional project). Programmes are usually employed for business transformation calling for an integrated approach inherent to change management. While the uncertainty of a project greatly depends on external project dependencies (mainly external products), a programme also deals with internal programme dependencies (or interfaces) adding to complexity. From a learning perspective, the implication is that ProwLO may assist learning across programmes, but taking into account internal programme interfaces, ProwLO may as well contribute to learning inside programmes if 'programme elements' can be treated as sub-projects or at least show some level of process consistency with a project life cycle.

Management of knowledge at the portfolio level, situated in line functions in which project context holds less, should be approached differently as to complement ProwLO. In many cases, such knowledge still relates to projects, yet shifts away from PKM, as a distinct engaging process, to KM in project-based organizations *not* defined by life cycle management, except the knowledge life cycle. The very definition of ProwLO helps to define such additional component – from a process and/or system perspective – by exposing interfaces and dependencies applicable to project-based organizations in terms of interdependent enterprise functions. This is ProwLO+ and not the focus of this book. Note that in project-based organizations where projects play a lesser role (i.e. support business as opposed to core business), this additional 'component' may actually overshadow PKM, being the dominant function. In any environment, the bigger the portfolio and the higher the budgets involved, the greater the strategic value of PKM, and with it a defined approach.

The second aim is to increase 'Project-based Learning'. Projects unfold as parallel performance and learning processes. Learning is a natural outcome of projects but it can be fostered by increasing the learning capability of project members and by providing a solution that supports learning across projects over time and inter-project learning when multiple projects are run simultaneously. In addition to these two goals, ProwLO tries to solve or mitigate three business problems (see Chapters 2 and 3) that are somehow related to KM (or better said, a lack of it) and common in many industries. Hence, the starting point is individuals and project teams, but the value proposition for business is ultimately the deciding factor, the business case for change.

In Chapter 1, the knowledge needs of project members in PRINCE2 projects will be elaborated on as to provide a setting and application area of ProwLO. In Chapter 2, the ProwLO process model is introduced, in which ProwLO processes run in parallel to PRINCE2 processes. The project life cycle shaped by PRINCE2 provides an ideal framework for integrating KM with PM. The following chapters elaborate every single ProwLO process as part of the process model. Every process consists of multiple activities with implicit and explicit interfaces to other processes and activities as to form a coherent framework. Every ProwLO process chapter includes implications for alternative frameworks to PRINCE2, and concludes with a table that suggests roles and responsibilities for every single process activity. This table may inspire a definition of best practice that can be applied in the knowledge application process, i.e. a practical use of ProwLO.

1 Knowledge/information needs *in* projects

As mentioned in the introduction, ProwLO makes a distinction between Project Management Information and Reusable Project Knowledge with generic value. Another, sometimes overlapping, classification is the distinction between knowledge *about* projects, knowledge *in* projects and knowledge *from* projects (Damm & Schindler, 2002). With regard to knowledge about projects, a distinction can be made between methodological knowledge (e.g. how to manage a project) and macro-level knowledge about actual projects; macro in the sense that facts about projects could be shared by multiple actors, including project stakeholders. Knowledge in projects refers to knowledge that is generated during the course of a project. This type of knowledge includes informal information, which is exchanged through e-mail, meetings, personal discussions, etc., and also project deliverables such as documentation. Knowledge from projects is essentially newly gained knowledge (or experience) as a result of carrying out projects. In general, methodological knowledge has generic value, macro-level project knowledge is very specific unless it leads to generalization, knowledge in projects is very specific but often lays at the root of knowledge from projects, and knowledge from projects only has generic value if it can be reapplied in different contexts, that is, projects.

The first category of knowledge, project management information, supports the effective execution of any project from a management perspective, including stand-alone projects, and will be discussed first. The second category, reusable project knowledge, plays a role in preventing reinventing the wheel, repeating of mistakes and closing knowledge gaps (at the project level in particular), and is not limited to project management knowledge.

At the organizational level, one may resort to reusable knowledge from project external sources for greater knowledge reuse.

PROJECT MANAGEMENT INFORMATION

Project management information can be approached from either a process or an aspect perspective. The most obvious aspects of project management are arguably its sub-functions, which in turn provide a basis for (cross-functional) processes, as defined in process models like in PRINCE2 or Praxis. In this section, three overviews of project management information are provided under the label of examples. These examples summarize project management information needs. The first two are based on the PRINCE2 process model, namely two processes. The third one is based on a commonly addressed and generic sub-function of project management, namely project risk management. It should be noted that PRINCE2 itself is a key driver for knowledge needs in projects.

The starting point of the knowledge needs of project members in PRINCE2 projects is the PRINCE2 processes. According to the PRINCE2 process model, every process consists of sub-processes (also known as activities) and output in the form of management products. Some PRINCE2 activities are knowledge processes, in particular those covering Lessons Learned (e.g. Capture previous Lessons in Starting Up a Project). However, PRINCE2 does not define an overall framework and does not address other types of reusable knowledge objects, other than claiming to be a collection of best practices.

Therefore, for each PRINCE2 process, there is a parallel ProwLO process (this is explained in the following chapter). ProwLO is part of a project's life cycle and based on a process model, same as PRINCE2. The ProwLO processes will be introduced later respectively.

Every management product is an example of a container holding project management information. This includes information that is not documented formally but instead communicated verbally, transmitted via e-mail, or even recorded on tape during proceedings.

The two defining characteristics of project management information are that its scope is limited to single projects and that it is the outcome of project management practices. In contrast, reusable knowledge is the outcome of knowledge management processes. This scope refers to the target audience. Neglecting other contexts, overall, PRINCE2 is a single project method, where project management information still has potential for reuse, either based on transformation (modification + knowledge claims) or simply by reference as an example. Also, within the project management information – the outcome of activity and knowledge application – reference to reusable knowledge is commonplace. PRINCE2 not only describes steps to be taken but also suggests content as part of the output that may relate to corporate standards and practices, including techniques and procedures for specific sub-functions of project management (such as Risk Management).

Note that project management information at the conceptual level (disregarding real instances and examples) is process knowledge inherent to the PRINCE2 process model. The PRINCE2 process is standardized and can be repeated and tailored. Hence, ironically, reusable knowledge lays the foundation for specific project management information. Interestingly, PRINCE2 claims to be a generic method(ology) for any type of project, in any industry (now that is a wide knowledge claim!). In practice, however, tailoring may be a necessity considering project and industry characteristics. In any case, application of PRINCE2 maximizes knowledge application of existing practice, resulting in standard project management information.

Project management information is, however, not self-evident. This can be best illustrated by organizations that have not yet adopted PRINCE2 or are in the process of changing their project management approach. For example, not every project manager keeps account of an Issue Log. In such a case, additional attention needs to be paid to the added value of such management product in order to make sure that it becomes part of a project approach that conforms to PRINCE2, at least to a certain degree. In other words, you have to sell PRINCE2 to key users.

In the following sample PRINCE2 processes, the most important knowledge needs, early on as a project unfolds, are addressed.

Example 1: starting up a project (SU)

Starting Up a Project is driven by the knowledge needs of the Project Board in directing a project. Before a project can be commissioned, the Project Board has to know whether the project is viable and worthwhile. So the primary knowledge need is business justification, which is a continuous need during a project's life cycle. The trigger for SU is the Project Mandate which is provided by the commissioning body, either corporate or programme management. The Project Mandate is then further refined to develop the Project Brief, the main output of SU. Based on the Project Brief, the Project Board may authorize initiation. It is essential to provide the Project Board the information they need for sound and rational decision-making. This information is assembled during a sub-process and includes the following:

- Role descriptions of the project management team to ensure that the right people are in place. By appointing people to these roles, all necessary authorities will exist for initiating a project.
- A Project Definition covering objectives and desired outcomes, project scope and exclusions, constraints and assumptions, project tolerances, users, stakeholders and interfaces.
- Outline Business Case.
- Project Product Description.
- Project Approach.

Another knowledge need addressed by PRINCE2 is Lessons Learned by other projects, corporate or programme management and external organizations. Lessons Learned may relate to management or specialist work. According to PRINCE2, the Project Manager should capture Lessons about weaknesses or strengths of processes, procedures and tools. More specifically, focusing on management knowledge, previous lessons may influence the design of the project management team, outline of Business Case, the contents of the Project Brief and the Initiation Stage Plan. Relevant Lessons are captured in the Lessons Log which is created in SU. Lessons Learned are reusable project knowledge and hence are discussed in 'Reusable Project Knowledge'.

SU is not part of the actual project. It is not a project Stage. At the end of this process, an Initiation Stage Plan is created that contains management activities necessary for the next process, Initiating a Project.

Example 2: initiating a project (IP)

Initiating a Project (IP) is a management process; it does not involve specialist work. That is, it has no direct relation with the project product. The knowledge needs in IP are mostly based on the Project Manager's role, in alignment with the needs of the Project Board for sound decision-making. Notwithstanding, technical knowledge needs are part of the process.

The Project Manager needs to establish strategies on how to deal with risk, quality, configuration management and communication, define project controls, create a Project Plan, refine the Business Case and assemble the Project Initiation Document (PID) which is used by the Project Board to decide whether to authorize the project or not. IP is the first management stage of the project and provides the foundation for the rest of the project, including base lines.

For each type of strategy, the Project Manager needs to know whether there are any corporate or programme management strategies, and standards or practices that need to be applied by the project. Also, for each strategy, the Project Manager is recommended to seek lessons from similar previous projects. In defining the Risk Management Strategy, the Project Manager may have the following knowledge needs:

- Knowledge about Risk Management procedures (e.g. Identify, Assess, Plan, Implement, Communicate).
- Tools and techniques that can be used.
- How to report performance in relation to risk.
- Most suitable timing for risk management activities.
- Roles and responsibilities for risk management activities.
- Appropriate scales to be used for estimating probability and impact.
- Guidance on how proximity for risks will be assessed.
- Different risk categories.
- Early warning indicators.
- How to apply a risk budget.

Not only lessons are useful to satisfy the above needs but also are more widely accepted best practices. Similar to Lessons Learned, Best Practices are reusable Project Knowledge, and are discussed in 'Reusable Project Knowledge'. It should be noted that in some organizations, Risk Management is usually performed by experts. In such cases, risk management could be regarded as specialist work in the domain of project management.

In defining the Quality Management Strategy, the project manager may have the following knowledge needs:

- Knowledge about quality management procedures (e.g. quality planning, quality control, quality assurance).
- Tools and techniques to be used.
- Roles and responsibilities for quality management activities, including checking links to the corporate or programme quality assurance function.

In defining the Configuration Management Strategy, the Project Manager may have the following knowledge needs:

- Knowledge about configuration management procedures.
- The issue and change control procedure.
- Tools and techniques to be used.

- Roles and responsibilities for the procedures.

In defining the Communication Management Strategy, the Project Manager may have the following knowledge needs:

- The communication management procedure.
- Tools and techniques to be used.
- Roles and responsibilities for communication activities.

In comparison, the Praxis framework also addresses specifications and blueprints. Both can be better qualified as technical knowledge, and hence do not fit typical project management information.

It should be noted that the 2017 Update of PRINCE2 has renamed the above management products and uses the name Approach instead of Strategy.

Example 3: project risk management

Explanation

Risk Management consists of Risk Analysis and Risk Mitigation. Risk analysis captures a list of risks and assesses probability and risk impact. Probability and risk impact are based on a scale, e.g. low, medium and high. Based on this approach, a table can be drawn. There are two types of risks: one type can be mitigated, the other one is residual even with countermeasure. Hence, the first type can be (partly) resolved, whereas the second type can materialize based on probability.

In PRINCE2, risks are captured in a Risk Register. So this Register should address analysis and mitigation by means of countermeasures. The Risk Register is initially formed during Project Initiation, but risks are first identified in Starting Up a Project as part of the Project Brief which feeds on the Project Mandate. It is important that on the outside, when the Idea is still in formation, by Senior Management or Customer and Business Case owner, risks are considered at a high level. If this is not the case, then Business Case Development is flawed, increasing the risk of project failure.

In project-based organizations, historical data can be combined to create a list of risks and provide knowledge on the effectiveness of countermeasures taken. Also, the matrix of Risk Analysis in terms of probability and risk impact can be adopted as an example of similar past projects.

There are arguably two types of Project Managers: entrepreneurial- and control-oriented characters. The former are inclined to take risk and disregard probability of risk. They often overlook Risk Management and thus require support from analytical Risk Managers. The latter, on the other hand, acknowledge and relate risks to project success factors and closely examine each single risk captured. The indicators they use are embedded in control procedures and processes. In other words, they are methodology-driven and use analytical skill to assess the effect of risk on project outcomes, project performance and quality of delivery. I can illustrate this with three examples. An example of an indicator addressing risks affecting project outcome, such as imitation by a competitor, is a highly competitive market. Identification of such a risk may explain negative project outcomes, prevent project failure or explain premature project closure. An example of an indicator addressing risks affecting project performance such as technological complexity is technological failure in similar projects. An indicator addressing risks affecting quality of delivery – poor quality being the risk – is the level of faults or errors captured in the Quality Log – level of faults being the indicator. So indicators help to identify risks and relate risk to project success.

Risk Management interfaces with Project Planning. The Project Plan has inherent risks, and risks pose hazards to Project Plan execution. The risks associated with planning include rework cycles and delays. Rework cycles are self-reinforcing based on fatigue and an ever-increasing risk of repeating mistakes. Disruption and delay then becomes inevitable.

Risk Management also interfaces with Project Definition, Business Case Development and Project Evaluation. The interface with Project Definition is based on the link between Risks and the Risk Log. The interface with Business Case is based on the link between Risks and the Business Case. Project Evaluation relies on the Risk Log for knowledge capture.

The philosophical dimension to Risks is whether they could be treated as Issues. This is not only a matter of definition but also management style. If one presumes they are different fundamentally, following the definitions 'A Risk is a source of danger and has a chance to expose the project to damage', and 'An Issue is an anomaly from Planning and materialized', then Risks are managed proactively, whereas Issues are emergent factors and faced in an ad hoc manner.

Distilling/defining knowledge needs

Organizations that lack a defined process may refer to functional descriptions from various sources like the one above – on project risk management – such as knowledge resources. It could be the first step in developing detailed process descriptions. Based on the brief summary of project risk management, a number of knowledge needs can be identified:

- What are the risks in the project?
  - What can we learn from historical data?
- Of these risks, which are residual?
- What kind of format is most suitable for risk analysis?
  - Does this format include probability and impact (as a check)?
- Can this format be captured in a template?
- In the context of risk mitigation, what are the potential, chosen and implemented countermeasures?
- As a decision-making process, why were certain countermeasures chosen over others, or what explains the lack of countermeasures?
  - What can we learn from historical data?
- Does the project management team know the difference between risks and issues?
- How does project risk management interface with other functions of project management like, for example, project planning, and what are the links?

REUSABLE PROJECT KNOWLEDGE

There are numerous knowledge types. Each type says something about the nature of knowledge or format. Furthermore, each knowledge type is subject to media (video, audio, text-based) which affects presentation and format. Some knowledge types are media-bound or can be best represented by a specific medium, and others are medium neutral. For example, Cases can be captured as text according to a Template, but can also be captured as audio based on a questionnaire derived of the same Template, potentially prior to written capture. In contrast, IntraKnotes are, in their essence, text-based notifications. Similarly, website and web pages can be best treated, i.e. promoted, via links.

Listed below are common knowledge types. This list should be regarded as non-exclusive. This list challenges the traditional view that it is difficult to define knowledge types unambiguously (Edwards, 1967). The knowledge types are based on popular concepts and can be distinguished easily despite their potential ambiguity.

- Alerts (informative announcements or notifications; at the organizational level, Alerts are per definition boundary spanning, i.e. relevant across projects).
- Attention points (key things to consider when confronted with new, challenging situations).
- Best practices (imply higher benefits as compared to other practices or absence of the practice in question; require some general acknowledgement for their status; may apply to methodologies, methods, techniques, incentives, etc.).
- Book/chapter reviews (books are generally credible sources of knowledge as they go through a rigorous publishing process addressing quality and market fit).
- Blog posts (noteworthy type of webpages; authentic, personally driven articles based on authority/expertise in the field, reinforcing that reputation).
- Cases (problem + solution scenarios rooted in experience).
- Case study (perfect format to make one or more cases based on historical data).
- Checklist (a noteworthy tool to make sure that an activity has been carried out adequately).
- Task know-how (complex tasks often require sophisticated solutions; may or may not relate to best practices and/or routine practices).
- Customer knowledge (any information that is relevant for future client engagements in the context of projects/programmes, motivated by relationship management).
- Common issues (problems that tend to repeat across projects).
- Design (a refined blueprint and anticipated outcome of planned activities; mostly restricted by requirements, which may be generic to some extent, and possibly affected by physical limitations).
- Estimates (enable more accurate planning).
- Follow-on action recommendations (rooted in experienced actionable knowledge, bridging experience accumulation with business process improvement, empowering project members).
- General domain knowledge (accumulated factual-based information related to an established paradigm, in the sense that fragments are intrinsically related and can be labelled, but not infallible as knowledge is *often* a social construct (no matter tacit or explicit) and can be falsified or become outdated; a specific example includes concepts enabling abstract thinking to deal with complex reality; another example includes success factors, e.g. linking project outcomes with anything else with impact).
- Heuristics (e.g. rule of thumbs).

- Incentives (may explain unpredicted project behaviour or with regard to project benefits address failed targets).
- Insights, articulated (mental models based on understanding, which sometimes can be rationally explained and thus captured as explicit knowledge, but, in a competitive world, are not shared easily).
- Notifications or 'IntraKnotes' (informative messages, peer to peer, across projects; in some social media called Updates; compared to Alerts, the latter have a greater urgency and are less generic).
- Learning assets (e.g. fluidbooks, espressons, z-cards, training courses, infographics, animations (Hemsley Fraser Group Limited, 2017)).
- Lessons Learned (knowledge rooted in positive or negative experience).
- List of options (key element in general decision-making based on the premise that there are alternative ways to deal with a particular situation; input for the Project Approach which elaborates on advantages and disadvantages of each option).
- Manual/Guide (guidelines on use of a system or method).
- Mind maps (a noteworthy technique for externalizing sub-themes based on a central theme in a tree-like structure based on hierarchy with multi-levelness and different directions for a graphical depiction).
- Method (captures processes consisting of activities).
- Methodology (a philosophical proposition underlying a specific method or set of methods, usually driven by principles and addressing thematic aspects of the method(s) in question often neglected in process descriptions for method execution; these thematic aspects not only enrich methods but also help to select a methodology (e.g. refer to selecting a particular methodology to conduct research, providing a foundation for a more detailed research method); the richness of a methodology can be expressed by a meta-model (see the next Knowledge Type) focusing on abstract relationships between elements of the methodology – in most cases, process elements as part of a process model (see, for example, Appendix II which briefly explains some evolutionary progression of PRINCE2 based on meta-models).
- Model (abstract representation of real phenomena, often used as a blueprint and foundation for a design; a meta-model is a 'model based on a model' linking constructs at a conceptual level only, disregarding specific examples of, let's say, a process or activity).
- News (new developments in specific areas of interest based on interpretation of significance, potential source of non-factual information, and generally subject to human manipulation for various ends).

- Practices (doing) rooted in approaches (ways of doing and the act of doing something) (tacit, closely tied to individuals; do's and don'ts are an explicit example; may relate to personal, team and organizational routines).
- Presentation slides (key points used in a recorded/unrecorded presentation, often provided with illustrations).
- Product/Service knowledge (knowledge about deliverables, physical results or intangible value-adding activities).
- Principles (fundamentals underlying more detailed practice),
- Process (has a beginning and end state, and, in the middle, transformation).
- Quick facts (statements that capture essential information for specific purposes).
- Quick fixes/Troubleshooting (a simple approach to problems and solutions as compared to Cases for more complex situations).
- Regulation (provides restrictions on how and what to achieve, usually externally imposed and legally binding).
- Representative example (typical example with generic value).
- Requirements (usually associated with the end product and customer-driven; they are a specialist knowledge type based on technical definition, a specialist process, but arguably an intrinsic part of project management (although not typical PM information), depending on the role of the project manager who may act as business analyst, typically associated with requirements management; some type of requirements may have generic value).
- Rules (written and unwritten rules enabling more predictive behaviour in given situations or general conduct).
- Scientific literature (diverse work that is based on scientific standards in terms of construct validity, internal validity, external validity and reliability (see Yin, 2003).
- Specific example (enables greater reuse in similar projects).
- Stories (chain of events held together by a story line (or an attempt), which captures the imagination of listeners or readers based on the principle of identification or shared history and or interests).
- Technique (a way of carrying out specific activities that needs skill).
- Template (a standard format aligned with processes that may need tailoring).
- Theories (conceptual frameworks that explain existing observations and predict new ones).
- Tips & tricks (precursor of best practices, sometimes lacking formal, organizational and extra-organizational knowledge claims).

- Tool (e.g. software, questionnaires, checklists, decision-trees; an umbrella concept for process knowledge artefacts).
- Website and webpages (embedded information usually centred around a common theme(s), characterized by hyperlinking and available on networks).
- Wiki article (collaborative medium for capturing domain knowledge in custom format, which is strongly influenced by conventions).

In the following section, many of the listed knowledge types are (or can be) incorporated into a new model that enables further differentiation.

Knowledge type creativity model

This section introduces a new model of knowledge types, called Knowledge Type Creativity model (see Figure 1). The model provides a stronger foundation for the knowledge types identified earlier. The model has two dimensions: 'medium boundedness' (on the x-axis) and 'content-wise interpretation' (on the y-axis). Some knowledge types allow greater creativity, and the model addresses this aspect by identifying four distinct quadrants, as a measure for creative potential. The importance of creativity, as a novel differentiator of knowledge types, stems from the fact that it supports mutual interests in the context of organizations for survival in an ever-changing world. Without creativity, learning becomes a repetitive process, and the ability to learn faster than your competitor – including the notion of knowledge production – may be the only sustainable competitive advantage if we believe management guru Peter Senge.

Medium boundedness is the epistemological dimension – a philosophical view of knowledge in which knowledge is subject to influence of format, and technologically or culturally motivated, which limits intelligent or creative expression. However, the very essence of particular type of knowledge may favour presentation in a particular format, rigid or not. It goes two ways, and the two merge. Low medium boundedness of a knowledge type does not necessarily imply 'greater' knowledge essence, and it only means that its essence is more independent from format. If we, for example, consider the knowledge essence of risk, we see that format plays a dominant role. Observation shows that Risk Management practices have led to standardized capture of risk and rigid documentation. In other words, these practices, often based on Risk Management techniques, have contributed to uniformity in logical representation as part of format in documents, as in Templates.

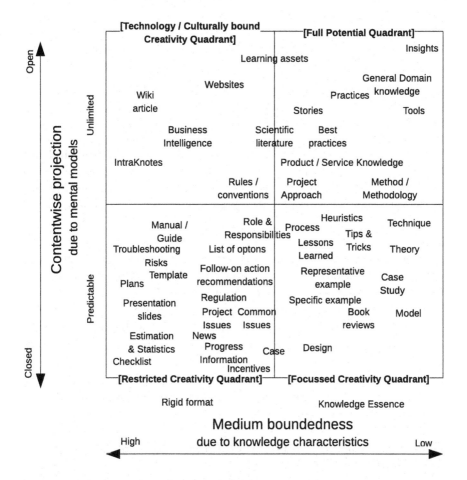

Figure 1 Knowledge Type Creativity Model.

Criteria for medium boundedness include:

- The level of format compliance as expected in organizational settings, based on format consolidation.
- Portability to multiple types of media *and* potential diversity in logical representation (i.e. semantic structure), as an indicator of knowledge essence that can be detached from format.

Content-wise interpretation is the human perception dimension. Interpretation as part of conceptual thinking is based on internalized views, such as mental models. Roughly speaking, open concepts are *associated* with greater purpose and diversity as opposed to closed concepts.

Criteria affecting perception, or rational grounds to perception:

- Perceived 'richness' of the knowledge type as a quality based on general conceptualization. Richness in terms of content diversity potential, in alignment with creative expression. Scope as a prefixed given, together with applicability, normally associated with the knowledge type, also plays a role. In other words, purpose affects richness.
- The level of potential reference to other knowledge types. The more the links and interconnectedness at both conceptual level and the level of real examples (instances), the less predictable knowledge with regard to content. And ideally irrespective of volume, purely based on intrinsic qualities of the knowledge type in question.

Building on these two criteria combined, for example, an IntraKnote with little information may be perceived as a more open concept in comparison to a large body of knowledge such as a manual that confines itself to a specific purpose and addresses limited topics (but any possible). Purpose or scope contributing to a sense of generic quality at the conceptual level should not be confused with generic validity of specific knowledge of a certain type across projects. For example, a Template may be useful to many instances of projects but has a very specific purpose (standardized capture of information in the context of specific processes), and is therefore highly predictable in terms of associated content.

Quadrant 1: closed perception and rigid format alias knowledge as usual

CHARACTERISTICS: CLOSED PERCEPTION AND RIGID FORMAT

Knowledge as usual is the type of knowledge that is both predictable and very standardized, often playing a part in routines at organizational level. Project Managers, especially older generations (pre best-practice era), are well known for having a very personal approach to project management, which contrasts knowledge, as usual, based on diversity (different ways of doing) and lack of formality (e.g. in filling out forms, ways of communication). In a way, this has a refreshing side but still is immature in our current rational understanding of organizational processes focusing on formal process definition and management. This implies not only potential conflict with organizational standards (see Chapter 5, section 'Knowledge Application', sub-section 'Standards') but also that PM practices are deeply influenced by tacit knowledge and cannot be standardized simply by introduction of Templates, Checklists and other forms without real resistance. This tacit dimension of project management is highly influenced by personal best practices. Consensus on knowledge needs may increase acceptance of process knowledge artefacts as part of the workflow. The challenge is to integrate personal best practices of project managers consistently with organizational standards widely accepted. This may entail modification of standards available in the public domain, often developed based on an approach that involves engagement with a community of experts. At the same time, projects demand – if we follow one of PRINCE2's principles – that project managers understand tailoring and scaling at the project level. This is an opportunity for personalization – in line with the spirit of project management as in essence – that needs to be governed.

Quadrant 2: technology/culturally bound creativity quadrant alias container knowledge

CHARACTERISTICS: OPEN PERCEPTION AND RIGID FORMAT

Container knowledge encapsulates other knowledge types, in particular those with greater knowledge essence, and is restricted in technical sense only through technology-inherent limitations and cultural conventions. Although technological possibilities seem endless and people culture is dynamic (opening applicability in multiple contexts), container knowledge is like a body without substance. Another metaphor is that of a mirror reflecting creative capability in the other three quadrants. For container knowledge to become more actionable without concession of creative potential, it has to be culturally embedded. Wikipedia technology in organizations is a success story in this respect.

Quadrant 3: focussed creativity quadrant alias specialist advances

CHARACTERISTICS: CLOSED PERCEPTION AND KNOWLEDGE ESSENCE

Specialist advances are the result of focussed creativity. Although this type of creativity may significantly improve project processes, the scope of every contribution is limited and relatively predictable. In general, specialist advances foster single-loop learning as opposed to double-learning and maintain status quo. For example, it would be an absurdity if a Lesson Learned would challenge the methodology it was imposed by. More likely, the Lesson Learned will address minor adjustments based on the principle of tailoring, such as found in PRINCE2. Notwithstanding, the essential quality of medium/format unbound knowledge combined with professional or academic excellence may produce groundbreaking results, such as innovative models, theories and techniques, as to the surprise of peers and public.

Quadrant 4: full potential quadrant alias disruptive innovations

CHARACTERISTICS: OPEN PERCEPTION AND KNOWLEDGE ESSENCE

Knowledge types in the full potential quadrant or near the borderline are the only knowledge types that may trigger disruptive innovations in the context of business. Such innovations are usually associated with new technology, disrupting markets. But in an organizational setting, disruptive innovations primarily relate to business processes and are concerned with competitive advantage, not so much with change in society due to technological advancement. The implication is that businesses may innovate based on unconventional approaches in every aspect of business. Business model innovation is a typical example. In ever-increasing competitive markets, affected by global forces, organizations first of all require a viable business model. Innovative business models enable new market entrants to differentiate at a fundamental level, essential for growth, while established corporations must ensure their business model is sustainable, which may require innovation as well. Note that the Knowledge Type model is relatively predictive, and hardly a full potential concept according to the Knowledge Type Creativity model, but in combination with market and product/service knowledge, plus entrepreneurial insight, provides the foundation of (the art of) Enterprise.

Generally, full potential concepts capture the imagination of organizational members, in the same manner as other artistic expression. This is evidenced by popular discussion of alternative project management approaches, mainstream engagement with Web 2.0 tools, promotion of best practices, etc. Similarly, the ancient concept of Stories contributes to sense making, which is a dominant theme in the post-modern organization. As business increasingly demands greater psychological engagement of people (Hirschhorn, 1997), due to the changing nature of work shifting away from physical labour, sense making may be the only profound answer to commitment, as to counter personnel turnover.

It is noteworthy that insights are the epitome of full potential in creative sense, but the development of insights is a function of ALL knowledge types. Hence, the model should not discriminate knowledge types based on value. Diversity adds to learning capability. Rigid formats are arguably also more effective in promoting organizational standards for greater benefit of knowledge exploitation. Also, unlike many process support tools, software remains a full potential concept (including the product itself). This is due to the flexible and wide scope of software (depending on requirements), the diversity of available solutions market-wise and, although in need of hardware, is not confined to a particular logical presentation as imposed by format.

It should be stressed that this model does not solve ambiguity of the different knowledge types, elaborate on their intrinsic relationships and that the position of individual types in this two-dimensional field is open to debate. In a way, it is a painting of relative positioning of elements. The model also requires additional validation of construct validity, e.g. by empirical research (a call for new research).

The added value of the model is more than a compressed depiction of knowledge types, and it enables a cognitive exercise in the philosophical search on the nature of knowledge. More specifically, the four quadrants may trigger the reader to reason how certain knowledge types are embedded or missing in organizations, taking into account creative expression as a fundamental part of work life, thereby adding to the contextual view of knowledge. From a knowledge processing perspective, however, the practical classification of knowledge types, as presented earlier, primarily based on reusable knowledge needs, is sufficient in defining a project knowledge management process, which is key in ProwLO. The philosophical aspects of knowledge, interesting or not, mainly serve as background information to provide a better context. Hopefully this will trigger critical thinking, only to realize, eventually, that ProwLO is the most practical approach to knowledge management, starting with the way it distinguishes and treats project knowledge.

2 Introduction to the ProwLO process model

Chapter 1 showed that management of project management (PM) information, inherent to a project management method like PRINCE2, is just one aspect of projects. The other key aspect is the management of reusable knowledge objects, which applies to multiple projects, adding a time dimension, and opening opportunities for long-term organizational learning. This chapter introduces knowledge management (KM) related problems based on such long-term perspectives. ProwLO provides a practical approach to solve problems experienced in practice to the benefit of business and greater satisfaction of knowledge needs to the benefit of individuals, a higher goal, not necessarily business driven. It is ultimately human curiosity that propels individual learning, with or without business incentives. Satisfaction of knowledge needs is included because awareness of needs, self-conscious or projected by others, is critical in treating knowledge as a production factor (analogous to other resources, requiring investment and management). In adopting such rational approach to knowledge, being an asset, managers will gain a knowledge management perspective in dealing with specific problems. Rational managers generally perceive business problems as challenges in need of systematic changes through rearrangement of tangible elements. Provided the means-to-end, any challenge is therefore doable if principally feasible, according to their philosophy. Most importantly, in the context of ProwLO's process model, knowledge needs drive knowledge processes which relate to the problems introduced in the next section.

KM PROBLEMS AS EXPERIENCED IN PRACTICE

If the vast majority of knowledge within an organization is produced and applied in projects, then the project organization should deal with knowledge processes formally, because knowledge production in projects, fuelling innovation, does not automatically result in knowledge exploitation at the organizational level. Many organizations mainly suffer from a gap between project-based learning and organizational learning. Second, knowledge application confined to projects, based on the type of business operations, has implications to knowledge evaluation and evolution over time. If projects deal with knowledge that has reuse potential in isolation, then the quality of that centrally available knowledge cannot be guaranteed and it risks getting out-of-date. A more fundamental problem is a lack of centrally available knowledge in the first place. In practice, organizations have addressed insufficient organization-wide knowledge integration. This includes concerns with regard to knowledge sharing in social contexts, in which knowledge is still bound to persons. So there is clearly a call for greater knowledge integration efforts.

ProwLO acknowledges the knowledge management issues as experienced in practice and provides a solution to management of knowledge with reuse potential. This solution is directed at solving three primary *business* problems, reinventing the wheel – in terms of products, knowledge (objects) and content in general – a very costly activity, repeating of mistakes (due to project amnesia), and knowledge/experience gaps. A business problem becomes a KM problem – in this order and to the interest of ProwLO – when knowledge processing can be used to deal with the problem, proactively or reactively. The first two problems are mainly rooted in knowledge integration and knowledge retention, and presume availability of knowledge at a certain time interval, or in case of the second problem, at least some kind of episodic project memory with reference to a mistake. The third problem may additionally raise the need for knowledge production – an aspect of knowledge management emphasized in second-generation KM by McElroy (2003). Spotting a knowledge gap depends on awareness of knowledge needs at three levels: the individual level based on a certain project role, project team level (group knowledge) and organizational level (across project boundaries). An alternative to knowledge production is outsourcing.

ProwLO obviously cannot solve turnover of personnel, another business problem with great impact on knowledge processing, but knowledge capture may mitigate knowledge and experience losses as insignificant as it may seem (a reactive measure). Dependence on key individuals, on the other hand, can be proactively managed from the perspective of project knowledge management affecting the magnitude of the problem. If a Master teaches his Apprentice well, he/she has a successor matching his/her skills or better. The Master–Apprentice model should inspire organizations to deal with the problem. Adopting a knowledge-processing perspective, the problem can be simplified to insufficient knowledge integration, most likely rooted in limited knowledge sharing by any causes, including cultural factors. The cultural dimension of organizations and knowledge sharing in particular is arguably a critical success factor for an effective, efficient and, above all, coordinated knowledge management process. Without a culture of knowledge sharing or significant drive to change status quo where knowledge is power, knowledge processing will have little or limited systematic benefits and technical KM initiatives will not be supported. In such cases, KM initiatives should be initially directed towards people and culture. Overall maturity increase may, in theory, stimulate cultural change – as in case of adopting ProwLO, higher maturity in organization and process, and in complementing ProwLO processes, higher IT maturity based on tool implementation. At the same time, management commitment will depend on maturity with regard to strategy and policy. Hence, ironically, management could be part of the overall problem.

Other problems like a gap between Project-based learning (PBL) and Organizational Learning (OL), project amnesia and insufficient integration of experiences in project processes also have a business impact but project members are less aware of them, simply because single projects do not impose a long-term perspective and the dominance of business as usual. Many of the mentioned problems are interrelated, as in cause–effect relations. Based on these relations, ProwLO acknowledges the latter three problems, together with personnel turnover and dependence on key individuals, as secondary problems, mainly amplifying the primary business problems stated above. Secondary status does not necessarily mean less significant. For example, integration of experiences in project processes is a key requirement for continuous improvement, a characteristic of highly mature organizations. For example, personnel turnover in combination with dependence on key individuals may cause overall business failure. It does likely mean that management buy-in for ProwLO as to focus on these problems is more challenging, as either their direct business impact is difficult to measure and elusive or there are alternative approaches to the problem (e.g. HR plans, competence development programs, etc.).

A specific knowledge integration problem worth noting is the difficulty to obtain knowledge in a timely manner based on knowledge pull. More specifically, finding knowledge artefacts or finding the right person who is the carrier of knowledge. Clearly, knowledge pull is driven by knowledge needs. But knowledge push is equally important in the context of learning and competence development, knowledge integration as a whole. The assumption that by fostering knowledge integration there will be less delay in knowledge transfer from a pull perspective is probably correct, but the question is how. In practical terms, a solution is required with retrieval capability regarding knowledge artefacts, but also a solution addressing socialization (in real life, virtually, or a combination) necessary for knowledge sharing.

After elaborating on the process model, all of the above-mentioned problems will be addressed once again, but now with a description in how ProwLO deals with every one of them. Part of this journey is to better understand KM solutions, and a conceptual model will be provided in Chapter 5. Instead of presenting a detailed theoretical framework of knowledge management first, providing a context for ProwLO, a conceptual frame of reference develops as we move from one process to another. This ensures that all relevant KM theory and concepts are practical (i.e. applicable to activity), situated (make sense within the scope of activities) and perfectly aligned with process-oriented project management. The latter principle is in conjunction with the key proposition of ProwLO, namely a parallel process model to PRINCE2 processes at a high level (!) and some key PRINCE2 elements at activity level (!), and will be elaborated next. Moreover, at this point in the guide, the most fundamental theories and observations related to knowledge and its management have already been introduced.

A PARALLEL PROCESS MODEL TO PROJECT MANAGEMENT

Project Knowledge Management as part of Project Management (not literally, see Introduction) is not a brand new idea as it has been coined a few times in the literature. The first one to address KM as part of PM was Chen et al. (2003) who conceived a collaboration project management architecture, inspired by two older models related to project management from a system perspective (mainly based on functions), which newly addresses the organizational level of KM in the context of projects (a great insight back then). However, the PM process based on underlying PM functions supported by this architecture lacks detail, consensus and, critically, does not address the integration of KM practices as part of the process. Inherent to the overall model (as blueprint for IT system design), the described KM component is a technical solution that enables project managers to compare or aggregate information across projects to derive patterns (as a combination knowledge conversion, creation mode). There are very few handbooks and guides that address KM in the context of projects. One is Nick Milton's (2005) Knowledge Management for Teams and Projects, but this book does not make KM activities a fundamental part of any process model supported by project management standards. And precisely this gap is filled by ProwLO.

Essentially, ProwLO provides a process based on a methodological approach (it works like a method with process descriptions), which is arranged according to a process model in alignment with project life cycle dynamics (providing the inevitable context). This leads to the following key proposition that makes ProwLO stand out in relation to any other conceivable KM framework (now and in the future). The ProwLO process model, consisting of inter-related processes, is a parallel process model to PRINCE2 with PRINCE2 interfaces at activity level. This means that ProwLO processes run in parallel to PRINCE2 high-level processes and that there are specific interfaces between the two. This creative approach establishes knowledge management as part of project processes and ensures that knowledge management is aligned with project management, sharing similar project life cycle dynamics. The project management environment plays a critical role in adopting KM practices. Without a defined project management process, the complementary added value of ProwLO is difficult to conceive. Partly because a standard approach like PRINCE2 makes clear – after contemplation – that PM strongly relies on process knowledge and its management. Also, ProwLO will not be effective without standard capture of project management information, based on the intrinsic links with reusable knowledge objects, but also because PKM depends on the habit of (any type of) information capture, which has cultural dimensions and other implications (e.g. with regard to strategy and policy). Thanks to the interfaces with (PRINCE2 based) project management, PKM may become more accepted (recall the natural tension) and successfully embedded organization widely.

ProwLO consists of 8 sub-processes, all unique in their essence based on the flow of activity in combination with implicit process goals. Figure 2 captures the ProwLO process model on top of PRINCE2's process model, directly mapping processes of both frameworks. The eight-process Post-project Knowledge Control is outside the scope of projects. This type of presentation, associating processes of both frameworks, not only stresses their compatibility but also makes learning ProwLO easier, especially considering that some

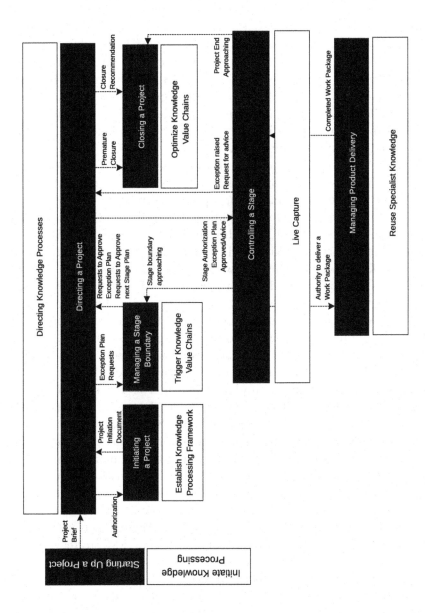

Figure 2 ProwLO Process Model.

ProwLO process names can be related to their counterpart in an intuitive fashion. For every single process, there is a chapter devoted, including an explanation of every sub-process (activity). The essence of every distinct process is briefly addressed below, by focusing on its meaning in relation to PRINCE2, which, according to the key proposition, provides a framework for parallel project knowledge management processes. It should be clear that every ProwLO process – except directing knowledge processes – is the main responsibility of the Project Knowledge Manager, a new project role as suggested for any PRINCE2 organization, purely defined by work as part of the process model, but as a distinct role not first introduced by ProwLO (e.g. Nick Milton used the term).

Initiate Knowledge Processes introduces a knowledge-processing perspective early in the project life cycle. At the time of Starting Up a Project, it is arguably more appropriate to speak of a product life cycle (if it concerns a tangible anticipated end result), focusing on the idea, its feasibility (a feasibility study could be part of SU) and a mandate for project initiation, in which project status becomes generally acknowledged. This knowledge-processing perspective raises awareness of support activity dealing with knowledge driven by needs. For everyone involved thus far in SU, this may contribute to a shared belief in which coordination of such knowledge activities is beneficial, if not paramount taking into account the organizational level. Initiate Knowledge Processes not only addresses satisfaction of knowledge needs in the specific context of SU for direct benefit but also establishes the role of Project Knowledge Manager as the main authority responsible for knowledge management in the entire project. Note that formation of the project management team is part of SU.

Establish Knowledge Processing Framework is concerned with the practical implementation of project knowledge management processes. While Initiating a Project in PRINCE2 focuses on setting up a predictable project management environment (in addition to other process goals), the ProwLO process adjusts this environment to the requirements of the ProwLO process model. Alignment is an important theme, also with respect to organizational KM strategy. Every single project, over and over, should address formal adoption of ProwLO as part of the project approach, first formulated in SU and later refined in IP as part of elements associated with the Project Initiation Document. This inclusion of ProwLO in project management information will ensure establishment of this framework, given the support by the Project Board in the context of project authorization and acknowledgement of other team members in general based on access to that type of information or more proactive involvement through communication.

Directing Knowledge Processes is essentially a sub-process of Directing a Project, a responsibility of the Project Board. This type of direction poses that the Project Board is a knowledge authority. There are two aspects to this. First, it means that the Project Board is knowledgeable. Most likely thanks to extensive experience and the seniority levels typically associated with Project Board members. Second, the Project Board already holds a position of authority, and therefore is in an ideal position to influence knowledge processes, taking into account both project results related to the delivery process and project outcomes, including less tangible benefits. So directing knowledge processes involves alignment with project goals. Since the Project Board is responsible for Project Assurance (delegated or not), it should be concerned with adherence to ProwLO processes. Like its parent process, Directing Knowledge Processes is based on key decision moments and ad hoc direction. But it is more focused on the overall headed direction as opposed to management by exception based on explicit tolerance levels following planning, principle to the parent PRINCE2 process. Following, assessment of the overall direction, in terms of knowledge processes supported by ProwLO, is more tacit in nature.

Trigger Knowledge Value Chains is a process triggered in the context of Managing a Stage Boundary, with roots in Controlling a Stage. The concept of Knowledge Value Chain is a key component of ProwLO's methodology. It will be fully explained in Chapter 3, but the basic idea is that knowledge processes engaging with a knowledge entity increase the organizational value of that entity. In an environment of recurring projects in which the principle of knowledge reuse applies (thanks to a certain degree of project similarity), the long-term value of knowledge may only increase if sustained properly, and thus, it is only logical to invest in knowledge processes as a whole according to a hierarchy of generic knowledge needs. The timing of Trigger Knowledge Value Chains is based on a reflection opportunity and new project information facilitating Stage transitions. As the next Stage is prepared with a new Stage Plan and an updated Project Plan, new knowledge needs may emerge. By linking these needs to the concept of Knowledge Value Chain, the organizational (not just project) value will not be neglected.

Live Capture takes place in the context of Controlling a Stage. While the Project Manager is in control of a Stage, the Project Knowledge Manager is in control of knowledge capture during a Stage. Obviously, there has to be an idea behind knowledge capture; otherwise, it will be perceived as an additional burden. Also, the process itself needs to be well balanced for greater commitment. In many cases, knowledge capture is a social process, and therefore, the Project Knowledge Manager should also be a motivator. But live capture is more diverse than the simple recording of knowledge as a few other aspects need consideration as well, especially those building on process interfaces.

Reuse Specialist Knowledge is situated in Managing Product Delivery. The latter process provides additional control of specialist work and an opportunity for the Project Knowledge Manager to get involved with specialist knowledge from a high-level position. Essentially, Reuse Specialist Knowledge postulates that projects may benefit from existing knowledge related to specialist domains (distinct from project management or any specialist PM sub-function). As the management of work packages as part of Managing Product Delivery interfacing with Controlling a Stage is pretty much a closed loop, the corresponding ProwLO process must ingrain itself for maximal effect. Although Reuse Specialist Knowledge depends on actual knowledge application by the specialists involved, the Project Knowledge Manager can evaluate reuse and do something purposeful with it. Hence, the reuse of specialist knowledge is rather a natural outcome of projects (a knowledge application process), but effectively manageable in the long term, thanks to real-time evaluation in actual projects (a distinct element of this process).

Optimize Knowledge Value Chains occurs at the end of a project, in the context of Closing a Project. It takes into account all knowledge value chains triggered during the project, including those that preceded the project (i.e. were defined in past projects), and optimizes them by definition of additional knowledge processes beyond the scope of the ending project and planning of corresponding knowledge activities. Optimization simply refers to maximum added value enabled by knowledge processes based on occurrence frequency and diversity. It should be clear to the user that different knowledge processes complement each other, serving different purposes towards a common goal. The different types of knowledge processes will be introduced as part of the Project Knowledge Value Chain in Chapter 3.

Post-project knowledge control relates to specific knowledge objects (captured knowledge) and, as the name suggests, it takes place outside the scope of projects. It is an ongoing process for specific knowledge needs that is potentially triggered by new projects, during and after their completion. Thus, the term post-project can be misleading, and a better characterization would be outside the scope of projects in which the knowledge need and object originated from. When new projects engage with particular legacy knowledge (of any origin), post-project knowledge control ensures knowledge evolution, a key principle in ProwLO. More specifically, after optimization of knowledge value chains, particular associated knowledge objects may need further refinement, and post-project control provides a mechanism to do so, first of all by collecting feedback in other contexts such as communities of practice (spanning multiple projects, relevant or not (ultimately in terms of knowledge application) according to project membership of experts).

MAPPING WITH OTHER FRAMEWORKS

Although ProwLO is fully compatible with PRINCE2, it can be aligned with other frameworks. Below is a mapping with two public domain frameworks and one commercial process model. Table 1 provides a mapping with the Praxis Framework. Table 2 provides a mapping with Project Management Body of Knowledge (PMBoK). And Table 3 provides a mapping with the ARCADIS process model.

Mapping with Praxis

The fact that the Praxis Framework is maintained web-based makes this methodology very agile, potentially satisfying all requirements of ProwLO.

Mapping with PMBoK

The interesting thing about PMBoK is the way the Stage-gate model is applied. In every identified Stage (referred to as project phase), all processes belonging to the key groups are executed, albeit some are more emphasized. In others words, if a project consists of multiple Stages, the cycles of initiating, planning, executing, closing and over-arching monitoring and controlling are repeated and scoped. Just like PRINCE2, PMBok acknowledges overlap of technical phases, but fails to add that phases not always coincide with Stages based on key decision moments (go/no-go). Unlike PRINCE2, PMBoK does not make a distinction between Starting Up a Project and Initiating a Project for a more controlled start. The implication for ProwLO is that Initiate knowledge processing and Establish knowledge-processing framework are combined. Another difference with PRINCE2 is that Directing a Project – a sponsorship equivalent – is neglected. Instead, PMBoK approaches project sponsors and other typical Project Board members as stakeholders and defines Project Stakeholder Management as a knowledge area for stakeholder engagement. In order to support the ProwLO process of Directing Knowledge Processes, PMBoK should

Table 1 Mapping with Praxis

Praxis process	ProwLO process	PRINCE2 process
Identification process	Initiate knowledge processing	Starting Up a Project
Sponsorship process	Directing knowledge processes	Directing a Project
Definition process	Establish knowledge-processing framework	Initiating a Project
Boundaries process(es) – sub-process of Delivery	Trigger knowledge value chains	Managing a Stage Boundary
Delivery process	Live capture	Controlling a Stage
Development process – sub-process of Delivery	Reuse specialist knowledge	Managing Product Delivery
Closure process	Optimize knowledge value chains	Closing a Project
Aspect of Governance process a sub-process of portfolio management, supporting the discipline*	Post-project knowledge control	Not applicable

* The suggestion here is to support any discipline according to the ProwLO process, including technical ones (not just management).

acknowledge a stakeholder process aligned with both Directing a Project in PRINCE2 and the former, because they are very inter-dependent (see Chapter 4). The impact of adopting such an overarching process like directing may in turn reshape the project life cycle in its entirety, resulting in closer resemblance to PRINCE2 and Praxis (the process models which are more similar).

Mapping with ARCADIS process model, a commercial context

What is missing in this process model is the Stage-Gate model in which key decision moments enable additional management processes, including the Triggering of Knowledge Value Chains. Also, Closing a Project is an not an explicit process. So the best alternative for Optimize Knowledge value Chains is Project Evaluation.

A quite unique Knowledge (from projects) Type of ARCADIS is 'Project references'. There is a special process dedicated to the capture

Table 2 Mapping with PMBoK

PMBoK process groups	ProwLO process	PRINCE2 process
Initiating	Initiate knowledge processing; Establish knowledge-processing framework	SU & IP
Planning*	Not applicable	Omitted since PRINCE2: 2009, repositioned Plans as a theme
Executing	Reuse specialist knowledge	Managing Product Delivery
Monitoring and controlling	Live capture	Controlling a Stage
Closing	Optimize knowledge value chains	Closing a Project
Not applicable	Post-project knowledge control	Not applicable
Aspect of project life cycle affected by organizational influences**	Lack of guidance for effective integration with Trigger Knowledge Value Chains	Managing Stage Boundaries
Not applicable	Directing Knowledge Processes	Directing a Project

* Planning is a continuous or at least recurring management process, but not all frameworks associate it with the project life cycle in an explicit manner. In the context of ProwLO, it is one of the many project processes that can be supported by project knowledge management practices (which e.g. may enable more accurate estimates). The process itself, however, does not trigger a distinct PKM process. There simply is no need to accompany planning with practices that relate to the management of project knowledge and, at the same time, can be clearly distinguished from elementary knowledge-processing activities (despite of being such a key project management function).
** Addressed but not identified as a process.

and retrieval of these knowledge objects, which are stored in central database. Project references can be reused for various purposes, including marketing (e.g. as examples in writing a tender). This process is another example of ProwLO+, bridging the project function with other parts of the organization (such as marketing).

The difficulty of the ARCADIS process model stems from the commercial/supplier environment in which this company operates.

Table 3 Mapping with ARCADIS Process Model

Project Acquisition (Tender & Mandate) P.1	*ProwLO+ process*
Resource Planning P.2	ProwLO+ process
Project Leadership and Project Management P.3	
Preparation P.3.1	Initiate knowledge processing; Establish knowledge-processing framework
Direction P.3.2	Directing knowledge processes
Tendering and Contract awarding P3.3	ProwLO+ process
Handover P3.4	
Project Execution (Advice, Design and Engineering) P.4	Reuse specialist knowledge
Handling Project documentation P.5*	
Monitoring and Control P.6	Live capture
Project Evaluation P.7	Optimize knowledge value chains
Concept design P.8	Reuse specialist knowledge
Complaints Claims Damages Recommendations for improvement P.9	ProwLO+ process
Not defined**	Post-project knowledge control

* This is essentially a 'reuse management knowledge' process. In ProwLO, this is not a distinct process, unlike the more isolated specialist processes as part of managing product delivery. Instead, it is an aspect of every ProwLO process, and flexible, depending on the formal project management approach.

** The management information system (see Chapter 5, Section 'Set Up Knowledge Management System'; Appendix I) containing process definitions and supporting resources is maintained by a content manager, but this maintenance process is not defined.

As a main contractor, it has to manage the supplier project (being the senior supplier, in PRINCE2 terms), as well as significant parts of the customer project or even the complete endeavour, starting from inception triggered by an idea. So, essentially, there are two project life cycles (possibly misaligned based on the moment ARCADIS steps in as contractor and takes control of project management as a service provided to the customer), driven by two separate business cases.

SOLVING THE PROBLEMS

The primary business problem of reinventing the wheel is mitigated by the capture and dissemination of experiences, web-based access to knowledge and use of standards. Only if you really know what you know as an organization, you can distinguish what you do not know. And when you combine this capability with identification of required knowledge, forming knowledge gap analysis, the chance of reinventing the wheel is minimized. It should be clear that as project members learn from experience and this knowledge becomes available to the wider organization, any organizational member will have a better picture of what the organization already knows. Access to centrally available knowledge makes knowledge gap analysis more effective, efficient and accurate. In contrast, fragmented knowledge, unidentified, is more prone to reinvention. Standards, on the other hand, impose routine practices which exploit existing knowledge and approaches. The primary business problem of repeating of mistakes is mitigated by fostering project-based learning, dissemination of Cases and Lessons Learned to the wider organization (thanks to web-based access) and Case-based Reasoning (see Chapter 5, section 'Knowledge Application', sub-section 'Case-based Reasoning'). The primary business problem of knowledge/experience gaps can only be solved with directed knowledge development or capture. ProwLO helps to expose such gaps.

The secondary problem of a gap between project-based learning and organizational learning is mitigated by the codification and dissemination of experiences; integration of IntraKnotes; by fostering reuse of existing knowledge; and by solving 'difficulty in finding knowledge', thanks to, for example, the proposition of a central repository of knowledge objects. The secondary problem of project amnesia is solved by the capture of experiences. The secondary problem of lack of integration of experiences in project processes is solved by fostering knowledge reuse. The secondary problem of dependence on key individuals is also mitigated by the codification and dissemination of experiences, in addition to standards. A people finder service, advocated by ProwLO, is another technology-enabled solution for the latter problem. Finally, the impact of the secondary problem of personnel turnover is mitigated by knowledge capture as a countermeasure for knowledge losses.

3 Initiate knowledge processes

The initial ProwLO process runs in parallel with Starting Up a Project. See Figure 3 for a graphical representation, which is based on a technique called Process Data Modelling (Weerd, 2006). On the left-hand side are depicted activities (process steps) and on the right-hand side the output is presented. The output side consists of (data) concepts, products or enabling technology. Most activities are meant to produce or update something. The same format is used for all the other ProwLO processes, in the following chapters.

CAPTURE KNOWLEDGE NEEDS

Every role, as part of the project management team, has different knowledge needs. These needs shape expectations as what to expect from other team members. So information and knowledge requirements play a dominant role in team relationships. It is therefore crucial that every team member is aware of the needs of others and that the team as a whole works based on similar practices. Adopting a standardized approach helps significantly in this respect. Additionally, socialization enables better understanding of each other's requirements. In addition, business roles in higher levels of the organization or different departments also have knowledge needs about the project, and it is the project team members' task to satisfy them accordingly.

Partly to conform to each other's knowledge needs and higher level management, contracts are signed by each individual project member (thus far in Starting Up a Project) in the form of Job Descriptions. Roles and responsibilities captured in these documents lead to activities that generate project management information necessary for the

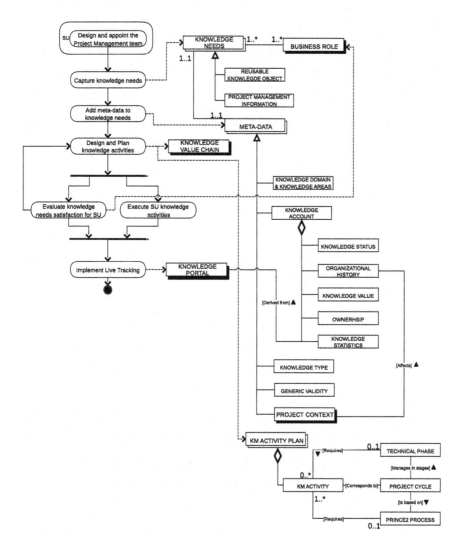

Figure 3 Initiate Knowledge Processes.

successful execution and supervision of the project. Socialization, on the other hand, also leads to the so-called social contracts for greater commitment to formal contracts.

At this stage, the process is characterized by limited information and lacks Authorization of the Initial Stage (and the Project as a whole). For example, there is no Project Plan still, there is just an overall idea of the technical solution/product to be developed, and there are no Specialists 'contracted' (i.e. assigned) yet. Hence, the main knowledge areas to be addressed in capturing the knowledge needs, following 'appoint and assign the project *management* team', are related to project management itself. This type of knowledge is essential for defining the Project Approach, also an SU activity. In any case, a simple categorization should be applied dividing the knowledge needs in reusable knowledge objects and project management information. The latter is based on the adopted formal project management approach and the personal approach of the project manager towards managing projects. His or her preferences namely determine how the adopted formal project management method is tailored and scaled to the needs of the project.

ADD META-DATA

Adding meta-data to knowledge needs provides the necessary contextual information. It applies only to reusable knowledge objects, which simply correspond to a specific need (one and the same) or *support* specific needs (do not fully satisfy). Knowledge serves a purpose and, without meta-data, it is more difficult to interpret the role of particular knowledge. Also, meta-data enables more search options and thus better retrieval in a system containing the knowledge.

Meta-data should first address the knowledge domain and knowledge areas (or sub-domains) based on simple taxonomies. A best practice is to use functions and sub-functions. For example, project management is a main function consisting of sub-functions such as planning, monitoring and control, project evaluation, risk management, and business case development. For a model of project sub-functions (based on a technique called Enterprise Function Modelling), see Figure 4.

Second, knowledge needs have a knowledge account. The knowledge account rationalizes the value of knowledge and provides insight on knowledge status. The knowledge account has five elements: knowledge status (e.g. existing, in development, in the process of evaluation, etc.), organizational history (roots and background), ownership (answers questions like: who is the creator? Who is accountable for knowledge quality?), knowledge value (why should one bother?), knowledge statistics (quantifiable value indicators).

Third, reusable knowledge has a knowledge type. The numerous types of knowledge objects have been listed in Chapter 1, section 'Reusable Project Knowledge'. An organization may adapt the different knowledge types based on a custom classification scheme, maybe

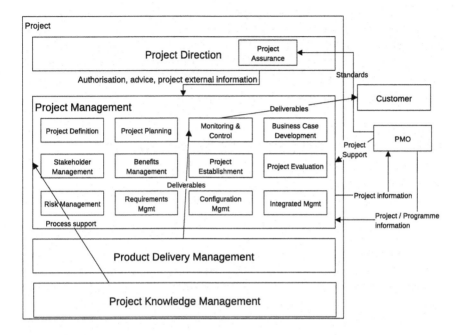

Figure 4 Project Functions.

to shorten the list or to align classification of knowledge objects with supporting software. In a way, every knowledge object addressing a particular knowledge type is a tool that can be used in projects, but types like Cases and Lessons Learned are fundamentally different from, let's say, a tool like a questionnaire, in terms of knowledge processing (e.g. how this type of knowledge can be captured) but also on epistemological grounds (i.e. philosophical views).

Fifth, reusable knowledge has generic validity. Reusability implies a claim that the same knowledge applies or can be reapplied in similar situations. The higher the generic validity, the wider the claim and more reusable the knowledge is. For example, if a problem captured as a Case occurs often, across projects, then it becomes automatically generic. It should be noted that determining generic validity is arbitrary and depends on expert judgement. The recommended scale is 1–5.

Finally, project context. As mentioned above, knowledge objects correspond to knowledge needs. More specifically, a knowledge object corresponds to a knowledge need in a specific project. This association needs to be made explicit by adding a project reference, that is, a project name and project id. If capture of knowledge needs is supported by a tool and automated (as opposed to plain documentation and document control), then project reference implies linking to a project entity. Context, however, is more than association. The project context should also address the role of knowledge in relation to project processes. Linking knowledge to projects enables the concept of organizational history of knowledge for future reference, which addresses the knowledge need across projects.

DEFINE AND PLAN KNOWLEDGE ACTIVITIES

It is natural for project members to acquire knowledge necessary for the execution of particular tasks. However, without a knowledge-processing framework, knowledge acquisition is project-centric (neglects organization-wide knowledge value), remains ad hoc (and may cause unexpected delays) and fragmented (as there is no body to deal with knowledge consistency and knowledge quality). Moreover, without a framework, projects will remain project work, completely ignoring other knowledge processes that are essential for long-term success of an organization. If knowledge activities are limited to people outside of projects, or even worse, not promoted at all, then project knowledge management will remain ineffective. It has to be a component of projects but with an organizational focus.

A knowledge-processing framework essentially consists of a number of distinct and generic knowledge processes. ProwLO suggests a model that is based on the concept of a knowledge life cycle and the notion of value-adding activities. The life cycle of knowledge acknowledges that knowledge is subject to change from its initial creation. As such, knowledge may evolve over time, e.g. due to changing circumstances (different situations may require different approaches), or eventually loose status and reusability (e.g. due to change in technology or simply no longer being considered as valid based on new facts). The notion of value-adding activities implies that the value of knowledge depends on its impact, which in turn can be manipulated by transforming it (e.g. knowledge evaluation may trigger knowledge modification and continuous improvement).

Figure 5 presents the knowledge-processing framework of ProwLO: the Project Knowledge Value Chain. It should be stressed that this model is essentially a modified version of Weggeman's (2004) value chain which includes elements of two other models, namely Becerra et al.'s (2004) generic KM processes and McElroy's (2003) Knowledge Life Cycle.

Knowledge Gap Analysis is a planned approach towards the discovery of knowledge gaps. It provides insight on what we know and what we don't

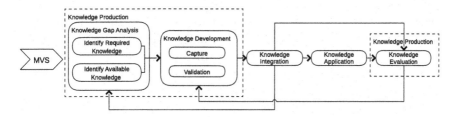

Figure 5 Project Knowledge Value Chain (PKVC).

know at both project and organizational levels. If you don't know what you know, then you might ending up reinventing the wheel (that could otherwise be prevented). If the latter holds, then it follows that you also do not know what you do not know (if you knew, you would be confident not reinventing the wheel). It is the same side of the coin. Knowledge gap analysis suits a purpose, namely it triggers knowledge development in order to satisfy a knowledge need. In order to determine what you know and what you don't know based on what is required, and thus conclude knowledge gaps, it is essential to identify available knowledge.

Knowledge Development is the development of knowledge objects triggered by knowledge gaps. This process consists of knowledge capture (externalization and codification) and knowledge validation (adding knowledge claims to codified knowledge). It should be stressed that there could be a delay between capture in projects and organization-wide validation, e.g. executed in the context of Communities of Practice (CoP) or the Project Management Office (PMO).

Knowledge Integration corresponds to knowledge dissemination (including knowledge acquisition which is intricate), within projects and across the organization, and highly depends on knowledge sharing. This process is supported by broadcasting, searching, teaching and sharing. The better knowledge is integrated, the higher its potential impact and chance of reuse, and thus, its effectiveness.

Knowledge Application is the application of knowledge in a business context, such as a project task. The actual use of knowledge is the best justification for its capture in the first place. It can be difficult, however, to predict its reuse in future projects. Also, in some cases, it could be essential to develop or acquire knowledge for the sake of the end product disregarding potential reuse. Knowledge application follows knowledge integration: it adds even more value and has real impact on projects.

Knowledge Evaluation is primarily concerned with the evolution of existing knowledge, but also with discovery of systematic issues and ad hoc discovery of knowledge gaps. Knowledge evolution is enabled by the possibility to modify and maintain knowledge. The deliberate search for systematic issues may lead to new innovations and better approaches. Ad hoc discovery of knowledge gaps is fostered by knowledge integration (as to better assess missing knowledge organization wide) and triggered by knowledge requirements as part of knowledge application and business processing (project work).

It should be noted that the knowledge processes are not per definition sequential. Figure 5 also depicts alternative flows or the so-called feedback loops. It should be noted that knowledge sharing as part of integration does not automatically imply knowledge capture (socialization may suffice), and knowledge development may be a natural outcome without prior *formal* knowledge gap analysis. In this context, natural means being triggered by ad hoc discovery of knowledge gaps in the context of knowledge evaluation, the final value-adding process, or project output directly related to primary project goals.

Compared to Weggeman's model, there are three major changes. In short, the combination of 'Identify Required Knowledge' and 'Document Available Knowledge' as the foundation for *planned* Knowledge Gap Analysis (not explicit in Weggeman's model). If not documented, available knowledge should at least be identified. Second, Knowledge development is viewed as the combination of knowledge capture (borrowed from Becerra) and knowledge validation (borrowed from McElroy). The third major change is that the process of sharing knowledge is replaced by knowledge integration. There are several ways to integrate knowledge, including broadcasting, searching, teaching and sharing (McElroy, 2003).

In defining and planning knowledge activities, the first step is to acknowledge knowledge processing for the benefit of the organization as whole and future projects. So, the first output of this activity is to adopt the PKVC. By adopting this model, the Project Manager will gain awareness of project boundary crossing knowledge processing and be able to better distinguish different types of knowledge activities.

After adopting the model, all knowledge activities necessary to satisfy the knowledge needs for Starting Up a Project are defined and planned (or at least estimated). This information is captured in the KM activity plan, which is maintained throughout the project. In SU, the KM activity plan serves as input for the Initial Stage Plan. Essentially, each PRINCE2 process and technical phase requires one or more knowledge activities. The project cycle based on PRINCE2 processes and corresponding to technical phases organized in Stages implies different knowledge needs during the lifetime of a project. Taking into account the project cycle, there is no point in defining and planning knowledge activities for the entire project during SU.

In defining a list of knowledge activities, taking into account the knowledge needs during SU and using the PKVC as frame of reference, it is necessary to perform a knowledge gap analysis first (sub-activity of the activity). Recall that this entails to compare required knowledge with available knowledge. Now that the initial knowledge needs are identified, knowledge gap analysis will reveal to what extent these needs are supported by existing codified knowledge (available project-wise or organization-wide) or can be attained (beyond the project) through socialization with or without exchange of codified artefacts.

Recommended SU knowledge activities include:

- Integrate PM Templates.
- Integrate ProwLO Templates.
- Refer to examples of Project Organizations.
- PRINCE2 activity Capture Previous Lessons (which is in fact knowledge acquisition).
- Refer to examples of Business Cases.
- Refer to examples of Project Approaches.
- Validate chosen Project Approach (compare with past approaches; generalization with organizational knowledge claims is not the goal here).
- Refer to examples of Project Briefs.

EXECUTE SU KNOWLEDGE ACTIVITIES

This activity is mostly self-explanatory. It should be stressed that all knowledge activities are either driven by knowledge needs of project members, and thus, are intrinsically motivated, or driven by knowledge needs of the organization as a whole or specific parts of the organization outside the project organization. Note that organizational knowledge needs are expected to be considered during 'capture knowledge needs' by taking into account different business roles but are limited to the context of Starting Up a Project based on the project cycle and to limit the scope. In many cases, the project management information created during SU will satisfy knowledge *about* this project by anyone entitled and interested. At this stage, little attention is paid to knowledge *from* projects with the exception of capturing previous lessons. All activity is aligned with finding business justification and preparing the first project stage: Project Initiation. Awareness of organizational knowledge needs by the project team might be raised to the level that members acknowledge that these needs are in fact a reflection of the needs inside the project. But then again they will not be bothered by any implications, especially knowing that the project must yet unfold. If, however, there is a similar parallel project facing the same challenges (disregarding phase differences) and that project members are aware of, knowledge activities could be extended to knowledge sharing from the very beginning. In any case, as the project will progress, it will become more apparent that knowledge activities are not limited to project management process goals but also take into account the interdependencies between projects (running in parallel and over time) and long-term organizational goals such as continuous process improvement in mature organizations. Consider a business case where a client wants to re-contract a supplier with whom he worked before in a past project. The client obviously has expectations and the question is whether the supplier can live up to these based on knowledge of the past project and access to similar expertise. So knowledge management is also important in the context of sustaining business relationships.

EVALUATE KNOWLEDGE NEEDS SATISFACTION SU

This activity is done in parallel to execute SU knowledge activities. If a bottleneck arises, e.g. due to knowledge being inaccessible or of poor quality, despite all planned and executed knowledge activities (according to the KM activity plan), then it may be necessary to define and plan new knowledge activities. So evaluation may trigger an iterative process. In this sense, this type of evaluation complements a planned approach towards the discovery of knowledge gaps followed by corrective knowledge activities defined and planned from the outset. Being ad hoc in nature and following knowledge application (i.e. project management practice) and simple enquiry or observation by the Project Knowledge Manager, evaluating knowledge needs satisfaction SU is in fact a knowledge process, namely knowledge evaluation at the end of the value chain also focusing on knowledge gaps (but now in ad hoc fashion).

IMPLEMENT LIVE TRACKING

Unlike PRINCE2 which is technology- and tool-neutral, ProwLO acknowledges that digital technology plays a key role not only in more effective and efficient knowledge integration (by better access, search capability, and incorporating context for better interpretation and more focused knowledge broadcasting) but also enables or facilitates specific ProwLO activities and supports other knowledge processes as well, namely every process of the PKVC.

In most primitive form, a tool is required for web-based access of all the different types of knowledge objects. The digital environment containing such objects, however, also needs to be maintained and the organization of knowledge is not a trivial task. Some ProwLO concepts – the counterparts of PRINCE2 management products on the output side – will need to be maintained in document format and hence will greatly benefit from document management functionality. The problem with most DMS on the market is that they do not support knowledge management and the full life cycle of knowledge. Hence, a combination of web-based knowledge access and document management is needed, either integrated or separate. An example of the latter is a Dutch multi-national engineering company that used a so-called management information system as resource for various knowledge objects (e.g. sample Project Plans) based on a custom process model alongside their third-party licensed DMS. In any case, the chosen web-based solution needs to support the full life cycle of knowledge.

By implementing Live Tracking, documented knowledge needs are made entities that can be traced and monitored in the system. If these project knowledge needs are backed by knowledge objects, it is possible to measure knowledge statistics that are part of the knowledge account. These knowledge statistics actually reflect knowledge processes in volume for specific knowledge types (see Figure 6 for an illustration

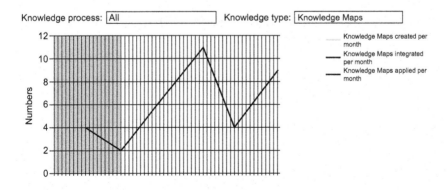

Figure 6 Measuring Knowledge Processes.

captured by a Knowledge Portal). By measuring knowledge processes, the value of knowledge suddenly becomes much more quantifiable.

As mentioned earlier, the project context (associated project), part of meta-data, associates a knowledge need with a project entity. All traceable projects sharing this need combinedly account for organizational history, another attribute. The Knowledge Portal should facilitate the underlying process of linking knowledge needs, knowledge objects and projects required for establishing a record of all relevant projects accountable for the organizational history of particular project knowledge. Without such cross-referencing and historical awareness, knowledge needs would be evaluated in isolation imposing barriers to knowledge evolution.

IMPLICATIONS FOR OTHER FRAMEWORKS

Table 4 Initiate Knowledge Processes Implications for Other Frameworks

PRINCE2 activity with ProwLO interface	Framework	Corresponding process element of alternative framework
Design and appoint PM team	Praxis	Appoint identification team
	PMBoK	Corresponds to the process of Acquire Project Team and Develop Project Team (as part of Human Resource Management)
	ARCADIS	Not defined as a distinct activity (of any of the explicit processes). Most related to ARCADIS' process of Resource Planning

SUGGESTED ROLES AND RESPONSIBILITIES

Table 5 relates roles to activities in Initiate Knowledge Processes.

Table 5 Initiate Knowledge Processes Suggested Roles and Responsibilities

Activity/ Role	Project Knowledge Manager	Project Manager	Project Board	1. Project Team Members 2. Chief Knowledge Officer 3. PMO
Capture Knowledge Needs	Elicitation/ Identification, Documentation	Reviewer. Primary source for identification of project management information needs	Reviewer	1. Potential interviewees
Add meta-data to knowledge needs	Producer	Reviewer	Reviewer	1. Review (as knowledge owners or potential users)
Design and Plan Knowledge Activities	Producer	Approve		1. Notified of involvement Acknowledge
Evaluate Knowledge Needs Satisfaction	Evaluation Either documented or communicated	Confirmation as key actor	Notified	–
Execute SU knowledge activities	Facilitate if necessary Participate if directly involved	Co-participate as key knowledge user	Support the Project Manager	1. Informed of knowledge developments 3. Potentially engage in activities (as expertise centre for PM)
Implement Live Tracking	Update IT system	*Provided with links (for monitoring individual knowledge needs)	Informed of live tracking	–

* This is an example of an information requirement based on a specific role in relation to an activity. In this case (and similar), a simple notification can satisfy the requirement. Note that notification events can be automated based on workflow software.

4 Directing knowledge processes

Directing Knowledge Processes is a sub-process of Directing a Project (DP). All sub-processes of Directing Knowledge Processes are sub-processes of (PRINCE2) Directing a Project activities. Also, all sub-processes of Directing Knowledge Processes are a responsibility of the Project Board. It is not a parallel work like the project knowledge manager role complementing the project manager as in the other ProwLO processes. See Figure 7 for an overview.

The fifth sub-process of DP, not included in the figure, is 'Authorize a Stage or Exception Plan'. This activity always follows Managing a Stage Boundary (SB), and thus, the parallel process of Trigger Knowledge Value Chains. Normally, Initiating a Project – the first project Stage – triggers SB. So if you take a look at Figure 7, there should be an SB process in between 'Establish Knowledge Processing Framework' and 'Authorize Knowledge Management Strategy', and accordingly an indirect flow from the former to the latter activity via 'Trigger Knowledge Value Chains' (instead of a direct flow). For simplification, these elements have been omitted. What is key in Figure 7 is how ProwLO processes relate to one another and the role of Directing Knowledge Processes as an important interface.

IDENTIFY KNOWLEDGE BROKERS

Based on the knowledge needs captured during Initiate Knowledge Processes, and other information like the Project Approach, the Project Board can point to Knowledge Brokers. Knowledge Brokers are intermediaries who bring specialists together (including producers and users of knowledge), thus fostering socialization. In some cases, knowledge brokers may provide knowledge themselves (based on

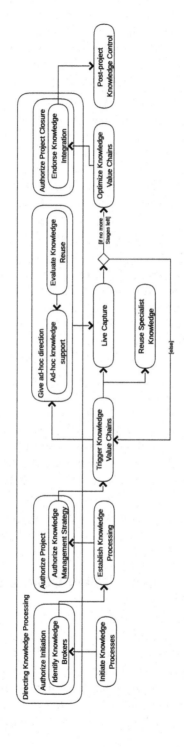

Figure 7 Directing Knowledge Processes.

mastery or being able to share it). The identification of knowledge brokers is based on the assumptions that the knowledge broker knows 'who knows what' and that the knowledge broker can introduce project members to these knowledge producers or 'carriers'. Another outcome of this activity, provided that the Project Board also knows who knows what, is that the Project Board may *recommend* individual project members to talk or exchange ideas with other organizational people. This is an example of matchmaking based on individual needs and a passive form of knowledge brokering (namely identifying the carrier).

During the project, in the context of ad hoc direction and knowledge support, it is not unusual for Project Board members to act as knowledge brokers themselves, simply by recommending or more actively by introducing people one another and proactive enquiry. But at this stage of a project's life cycle, the Project Board looks at other agents potentially able to fulfil this role. The primary knowledge broker is the internal project knowledge manager because he or she is part of the project team and develops a clear picture of all arising knowledge needs in the project. Furthermore, this person could be involved in multiple projects at the same time as in matrix organization providing specialist PKM expertise (in practice, we also see this for risk management). Combined with excellent networking skills, the project knowledge manager is the perfect bridging authority. However, there could be more than one project knowledge manager in the organization depending on portfolio size. In that case, the Project Board could easily identify multiple actors as Knowledge Brokers as first point of contact to reach specialists isolated from the current project and individual social networks. Note that individual social networks inside organizations are affected by geographical distance and physical barriers such as offices. Knowledge brokers are not necessarily project knowledge managers; well-connected project managers and specialists are viable candidates.

AUTHORIZE KNOWLEDGE MANAGEMENT STRATEGY

Part of Authorizing a Project based on the Project Initiation Plan should be to authorize the Knowledge Management Strategy. Hence, the latter should be attached to the PID so that the Project Board can make a decision at the right moment and in a broader context along with other relevant strategies (approaches) included in the same document. The knowledge management strategy should be aligned with the corporate strategy and policy on knowledge management (if available), and this should be checked by the Project Board. The contents of the Knowledge Management Strategy will be discussed in the next chapter, but adopting ProwLO processes should be part of this strategy. By accepting a KM strategy that includes ProwLO, the Project Board agrees to allocate time and resources for knowledge activities that are not directly related to project goals and objectives but still add value to organizational goals and strategy. Therefore, Schindler and Eppler (2003) advocate that the Project Board should agree to integrate learning and knowledge goals into project goals, primarily contribution to the knowledge base. Traditionally, project outcomes are anticipated in terms of physical and 'tangible' results. Note that knowledge objects (founded on data) and knowledge processes can be measured, as proposed by ProwLO, a rather tangible phenomenon. If, however, there is no senior support of KM practices (with or without corporate KM strategy), business pressure will not tolerate activities that relate to any scope other than the project. In such a case, the business culture will be dominated by time and cost. The other implication of authorizing a ProwLO-based KM strategy is a feasibility check. A KM strategy advocating ProwLO could be desirable and the Project Knowledge Manager knowledgeable, but not feasible in the context of the organization. Senior support and a corporate KM strategy are just the beginning. What is required is a fundamental KM infrastructure that enables KM systems supporting knowledge processes. This infrastructure consists of five components including: 1) organizational culture, 2) organizational structure, 3) IT infrastructure, 4) common knowledge (for shared understanding) and 5) physical environment (Becerra et al., 2004). This means that effective project knowledge management depends on basic organizational characteristics or preconditions and following overall organizational maturity. If there is a significant flaw somewhere in the infrastructure, the boundary crossing knowledge-processing framework (formalized and triggered by ProwLO) could be jeopardized. Note that the type of infrastructure may simply favour a different KM strategy. For example, the organizational culture, partly influenced by the type of business environment, could be more attuned to individualized-personalization (see Chapter 5, section 'Prepare KM Strategy', sub-section 'Boh's Framework'), and combined with one physical office where everyone meets; this could be at the expense of institutionalized-codification inherent to ProwLO despite offering a solution to e.g. 'Project Amnesia'. Provided that a supportive infrastructure exists (with the right people, technology and structures), the next challenge is to align ProwLO with existing KM systems, in particular with an IT tool. If an organization has to yet implement a Knowledge Portal focused on project knowledge, then ProwLO will have significantly less impact in terms of knowledge processes, and thus, it could be concluded that project knowledge management overhead is not worthwhile. In conclusion, this activity by the Project Board is a safeguard for organizational alignment in terms of project and organizational KM. It should be stressed that the current situation (As-Is) should not inhibit organizational change necessary for more effective project knowledge management. Organizations should be able to innovate and try new approaches in projects. The Project Board may, however, conclude that the organization is not ready.

AD HOC KNOWLEDGE SUPPORT

Ad hoc knowledge support as part of ad hoc direction by the Project Board addresses *emerging* knowledge needs of project members during the execution of a Stage that are raised by either Project Manager or Project Knowledge Manager. It is not a common practice that individual project members directly approach the Project Board (it might even be ruled out following the PRINCE2 hierarchy and strict lines of communication). In PRINCE2, ad hoc direction is triggered by requests for advice or provided when informal guidance is required to deal with different situations. Obviously, in some situations, this may involve knowledge exchange, but it focuses on the relation of the Project Manager (being the actor) and Project Board (being the guide), not individuals lower in the hierarchy. In ProwLO, the Project Board is concerned with (but not to the extent of being responsible for the provision of) *specialist* knowledge (in any domain, technical or management) as well. If the Project Board is unable to resolve the knowledge need, it can still act as a knowledge broker (as stated in the previous section 'Authorize Knowledge Management Strategy'). Second, the pretext for knowledge support by Project Board does not coincide with all the triggers for ad hoc direction. Examples of situations that may trigger ad hoc direction include (Litten, 2017) responding to requests, clarification, conflict resolution, responding to reports or external influences, individual concerns or responding to changes. Not each of these situations implies satisfaction of a knowledge need. Also, in some cases, it is possible that the Project Board uses its authority to direct without transferring the knowledge underlying the direction (as a sort of command), for example, by not providing arguments or explanation. In that way, the Project Board affects knowledge application. Emerging knowledge needs are driven by work in progress (real-time ad hoc discovery of knowledge gaps) but also by Live capture (of knowledge) while executing the stage, which is affected by planned discovery of knowledge gaps at the beginning of this ProwLO process (see Chapter 7). Live capture mainly takes into account organizational knowledge needs and triggers knowledge gap analysis at individual and project levels for every Stage. So Live capture both exposes project external knowledge needs that relate to the current project and identifies knowledge needs based on Stage foresight. The latter depends on the results of Managing a Stage Boundary, early activities in Live capture that co-shape the process of knowledge capture (corresponding to the planned discovery of knowledge gaps as stated above), and on general knowledge about projects, including technical phases, triggered by Stage engagement.

EVALUATE KNOWLEDGE REUSE

Evaluate Knowledge reuse is also a sub-process of ad hoc direction and may trigger ad hoc knowledge support. Its sole purpose is to increase knowledge reuse by raising awareness, thanks to the Project Board. Evaluate knowledge reuse is a continuous process during Stages, across Stages but has *formally* no direct event or time trigger. It simply follows the authorization of a Stage or Exception Plan. So to really put this into practice, the Project Board has to be willing to conduct this activity and have the discipline to find a moment and perform this while facing acute project challenges during every Stage requiring special attention. A recommended potential trigger, however, is when the Project Board evaluates Highlight Reports as a Stage unfolds. Based on new feeds and signs, the Project Board may decide to reflect on the actual relation between project performance and knowledge reuse (the exploitation of available knowledge across the organization). The motive could be a project that is underperforming or a need for project acceleration. Evaluation of knowledge reuse involves analysis between, on the one hand, identified knowledge needs and corresponding knowledge value chains (mainly data delivered or made available by the Project Knowledge Manager) and, on the other hand, available knowledge that is actually being applied in the project (as can be observed from project deliverables and project management information), from any available source, and contrast this with knowledge available organization wide. The central questions are: What do they need? What do they use? And what is available? The Project Board will most likely focus on generic knowledge they are readily aware of and that is somehow omitted in the current project, but also on specific knowledge they are less familiar with but which appears to be critical on closer look. In either case, the Project Board may engage (or trigger) in searching knowledge to find knowledge objects that support the initial knowledge needs (documented or not) and present the results to the Project and Project Knowledge Manager, who subsequently may apply the knowledge or act as Knowledge Broker to the rest of the team.

One special area of interest is the application of knowledge gained during the project at an earlier stage taking into account project duration. For lengthy projects, a potential pitfall is project amnesia, which is relevant across projects. Live capture addresses this problem, but also increases understanding of complex matters based on reflection and dialogue. Newly gained knowledge could be essential to resolve Cases and Issues. It could also prevent the repeating of mistakes within one single project. Subsequently, the Project Board could pay attention to captured Cases to check whether the responsible figures were able to learn from project events and behaviour and take advantage of these lessons in the form of successful countermeasures. It should be understood that Cases are not only useful for historical purposes and are limited to retrospection but can be used proactively for decision-making based on the fact that problems tend to repeat themselves or simply continue despite initial countermeasures. In other words, the initial response to a problem is often ineffective as the decisions and actions that follow rarely live up to expectations or result in desired outcomes. The root causes are bounded rationality and complexity of phenomena (problems are mostly the result of a combination of factors and their interplay which is difficult to grasp from the very beginning). The only way to become more effective from the start is to accumulate experience or apply experience gained by others. If the project team has to rely on their own expertise, then it should strive for the ability to resolve problems enabled by individual learning capability, the iterative character of problem solving (the possibility to try new things and wait for the outcome), and a well-documented process of problem solving and project behaviour which prevents project amnesia and fosters reflection and dialogue, and in turn, learning in a social context. The Case-method which will be introduced in Chapter 5, section 'Knowledge Capture', sub-section 'Cases-method' is the perfect tool for proactive decision-making in an iterative context and of course provides a means to capture valuable historical knowledge that can be reused in similar scenarios in future projects. Familiarity of certain Cases – captured in other projects – by the Project Board makes evaluation of knowledge reuse more profound and, more importantly, could trigger ad hoc knowledge support by initiative of the Project Board. The same applies to other types of reusable knowledge.

As part of the evaluation, the Project Board may consider four – but not unambiguous – situations of knowledge reuse as identified by

Markus (2001) in her theory on knowledge reuse. The same applies to the Project Knowledge Manager, but in different ProwLO activities described in this book. The four generic situations are 'shared work producers', 'shared work practitioners', 'expertise-seeking novices' and 'secondary knowledge miners'. The difference between the first two is that shared work producers create knowledge for their own later reuse, while shared work practitioners create knowledge for each other's reuse, doing similar work in different contexts. In the context of ProwLO, project team members are principally shared work producers as they anticipate knowledge reuse in the current or future projects, by themselves or other team members. But they are also shared work practitioners at organizational level (and beyond) being part of a Community of Practice. This situation is different in the sense that the project context is less obvious. Although shared work practitioners may lack context for total understanding of new knowledge, being unfamiliar with specific situations, they still can relate to it. This proposition applies to knowledge reuse at the organizational level in general. Markus argues that the four distinct knowledge reuse situations imply different requirements with regard to knowledge repositories. In a commercial context, this means that they are different types of Tool users and Use Cases.

ENDORSE KNOWLEDGE INTEGRATION

The Project Board authorizes Project Closure at the end of the final Stage or premature closure, triggered by closure recommendation, either naturally provided by the Project Manager near the project's planned end or forced by Project Board's influence in the context of ad hoc direction. Both cases are rooted in the Closing a Project process. This is the final activity of the Project Board and a perfect occasion for the Project Board to become directly involved with the project's knowledge value chains, created or adopted, and finally optimized in parallel project knowledge management proceedings relative to Closing a Project. This involvement is straightforward, namely to endorse reusable knowledge objects applied in the project, newly created or reused. The key is to make a selection taking into account the degree particular knowledge satisfies organizational needs and its overall value, which is a function of factors like potential reusability (in terms of frequency and generic validity, i.e. the level of application in different scenarios), measured knowledge processes, quality (i.e. internal validity in terms of solid knowledge claims, consistency of language, and false information in general), and interpretation of the specified knowledge value as part of the knowledge account of the corresponding knowledge need (see meta-data of knowledge objects). By endorsing knowledge (as in liking or recommending, or simply endorsing in social media), the Project Board adds credibility which in turn may affect knowledge processes, including evaluation, integration and application. That is to say, endorsement may increase interest in communities of practice and future projects, subsequently leading to more activity linked to these knowledge objects. To promote such amplification of knowledge processes based on a position of authority is basically a great tribute to knowledge value chains by the Project Board.

IMPLICATIONS FOR OTHER FRAMEWORKS

A key limitation of PMBoK is that it does not define a sponsorship (i.e. project board) process group. All the process groups and knowledge areas of this body of knowledge address the project management level of projects, from the viewpoint of project managers. While Project Board decisions are driven by process activities executed by the Project Manager, they do not stand out in PMBoK. PMBoK also provides limited guidance on the Project Organization, a key feature of the PRINCE2 method, which highlights the role of the Project Board. It does acknowledge the function of Project Governance and positions the project sponsor as both a stakeholder and member of the project team. It should be noted that a key feature of PMBoK, the so-called nine knowledge areas, which are applied in the different process groups, offers an interesting model for development of competences. Stanisław Gasik (2011), who followed PMBoK principles, developed Project Knowledge Management as another complementary knowledge area (aligned with the rest of PMBoK), a worthy read.

Situated in a commercial context, the ARCADIS process model has the same issue. One possible reason why directing a project is left out could be the customer and project owner largely define how a project needs to be managed. Another reason is that ARCADIS is not always responsible for the entire project but parts of it, while Directing a Project is based on the entire project life cycle. On the other hand, the PRINCE2 Directing a Project activities are quite universal and almost always happen, with the exception of a controlled start marked by Authorize Initiation.

Table 6 relates Directing Knowledge Processes with the Praxis Framework, PMBok and the ARCADIS process model.

Table 6 Directing Knowledge Processes Implications for Other Frameworks

PRINCE2 activity with ProwLO interface	Framework	Corresponding process element of alternative framework
Authorize Initiation	Praxis	Review request for authorization, as to proceed with the definition phase (Initiation Stage in PRINCE)
	PMBoK	The start-up phase (not a PRINCE2 project stage) precedes Initiating processes. So, Authorize Initiation or equivalent is not a formal part of the PMBoK process model. PMBoK does depict that the Initiating Proces Group relies on a project statement of work, a business case and agreements, but this is too limited as to expect that PMBoK will trigger the ProwLO activity of 'Identify Knowledge Brokers'. Particularly, the definition of a project management team, perhaps combined with identification of key specialists, is an important precondition because knowledge brokering becomes practical only if key roles and responsibilities are clarified and allocated to real individuals
	ARCADIS	In situations where ARCADIS takes responsibility for the management of the entire project, it could apply PRINCE2 in practice, provided it is empowered legally. This especially holds for projects with ARCADIS involvement early in the process getting this opportunity, either during the start-up phase (idea development, feasibility studies, etc.) or PRINCE2 initiation stage, following start-up, specifically designed to define and set up a project management environment
Authorize Project	Praxis	Review request for authorization, as to proceed with a stage or tranche (there is no explicit reference to project authorization)
	PMBoK	The project is formally authorized based on the Project Charter, the outcome of 'Develop project charter'
	ARCADIS	ARCADIS has a well-defined process for project acquisition, which provides authorization for the internal project. For the customer project, it needs an additional framework like PRINCE2

(*Continued*)

Table 6 (Cont.)

PRINCE2 activity with ProwLO interface	Framework	Corresponding process element of alternative framework
Give ad hoc direction	Praxis	Provides management support as defined, with explicit knowledge support. Evaluation of knowledge reuse is an additional responsibility
	PMBoK	With a clear sponsorship process missing, PMBoK does not provide enough attention to project management support. Therefore, ad hoc knowledge support cannot be guaranteed. The same applies to 'Evaluation of knowledge reuse'. There is no quick fix for this lack, so it is in the interest of ProwLO to tailor PMBoK to include a sponsorship process just like the one in PRINCE2, in which life cycle management of projects is characterized by different layers of management
	ARCADIS	As main contractor, the role of ARCADIS coincides with the role of the Senior Supplier as part of the Project Board. In this role, ARCADIS should set an example and take into account ProwLO requirements
Authorize Project Closure	Praxis	Confirm closure as defined, complemented with the activity of 'Endorse Knowledge Integration' for greater organizational benefits of knowledge dissemination
	PMBoK	Authorize Project Closure is not an explicit process activity in PMBoK but it is universal. With little effort, a reference could be added to 'Endorse Knowledge Integration'
	ARCADIS	Closing the customer project formally is an essential requirement in any commercial context. Following the PRINCE2 organizational structure, there are multiple organizations represented in the Project Board, which has implications for the ProwLO activity of 'Endorse Knowledge Integration'. Knowledge integration driven by ARCADIS as Senior Supplier should primarily target the ARCADIS organization. Knowledge sharing with the customer representatives, or other relevant cross-organizational contexts, is of secondary importance and should be approached with caution (due to confidential

(*Continued*)

Table 6 (Cont.)

PRINCE2 activity with ProwLO interface	*Framework*	*Corresponding process element of alternative framework*
		matters and the strategic value of knowledge). In specific cases, it might be desirable to exchange knowledge and learning outcomes in order to develop a long-term relationship with the customer based on trust

SUGGESTED ROLES AND RESPONSIBILITIES

Table 7 relates roles to activities in Directing Knowledge Processes.

Table 7 Directing Knowledge Processes Suggested Roles and Responsibilities

Activity/Role	*Project Knowledge Manager*	*Project Manager*	*Project Board*	*1. Project Team Members 2. Chief Knowledge Officer 3. PMO*
Identify Knowledge Brokers	Engage/ establish a relationship with the Project Board. Goal is to trigger this activity and promote the Project Board's role*	Observation	Facilitate networking. Make introductions	–
Authorize Knowledge Management Strategy	Develop Knowledge Management Strategy	Provide details to the Project Board	Authorize KM strategy as part of the Project Initiation Document	2. Notified of accepted KM strategy in case of project authorization

(*Continued*)

Table 7 (Cont.)

Activity/Role	Project Knowledge Manager	Project Manager	Project Board	1. Project Team Members 2. Chief Knowledge Officer 3. PMO
Ad hoc Knowledge Support	Observation Communicate observations with Project Manager	Knowledge pull as knowledge user and knowledge push as to compensate project hierarchy**	Provide	1. Receives direct or indirect support, thanks to knowledge brokering of the Project (Knowledge) Manager
Evaluate Knowledge Reuse	Gets informed as an arrangement with the Project Board	Gets informed on the outcome, proactively approach board members based on individual knowledge needs	Evaluate	2. Gets informed via the Project Knowledge Manager
Endorse Knowledge Integration	Engage with the Project Board near project end as to stress the importance of this activity	Reflect and discuss key knowledge assets with Project Knowledge Manager	Endorse knowledge	3. Facilitate electronic Knowledge Endorsement based on simple guidelines on use

* It is interesting to observe how the relationship between Project Board and the Project Knowledge Manager may evolve in practice, with Project Managers in the middle.
** Formal hierarchy and strict lines of communication may prohibit the Project Board to directly support key actors, management or specialist. The Project Manager may act here as a knowledge broker.

5 Establish knowledge processing (framework)

Establishing Knowledge Processing is the Project Knowledge Manager's equivalent of Initiating a Project and runs in parallel to the latter PRINCE2 process (see Figure 8). Compared to Initiating Knowledge Processes, this process has greater external orientation (seeks alignment with the organizational context) and is a means to institutionalize project knowledge management (based on formal authorization of ProwLO as part of the project approach). Initiating Knowledge Processes is limited to the introduction of knowledge as objects that can be manipulated like data and strongly rely on technology (a Knowledge Portal for Live tracking) and focuses on knowledge needs satisfaction during this initial project process, implying the need for planning and executing knowledge activities, and setting an example for the rest of the project. In short, it triggers knowledge processes at a very initial stage, even introducing the concept of a project knowledge value chain, but does not communicate an overarching coherent framework. The wider picture is potentially still missing for all project members, excluding the Project Knowledge Manager qualified in ProwLO. This wider picture is undoubtedly provided by Establishing Knowledge Processing, which elaborates on project knowledge management as project boundary spanning process and ensures that ProwLO truly becomes integrated with the project management framework for the current project. Just like with PRINCE2, there has to be a common language and this is perfected during Establishing a Knowledge Processing Framework.

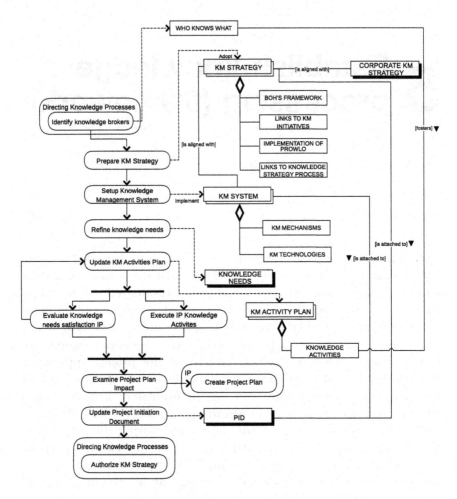

Figure 8 Establish Knowledge Processing Framework.

PREPARE KM STRATEGY

Prepare KM strategy follows Authorization of Project Initiation, including Identification of Knowledge Brokers. The KM strategy, in fact, is an extension of the Project Approach that is added to the Project Initiation Document at the end of this ProwLO process. Note that the PID complements the Project Approach by addressing various strategies. The KM strategy consists of four elements, which are described in the following sub-sections.

Boh's framework

The first element of the KM strategy states the primary knowledge management strategy of the organization as a whole, making a distinction – if there is a difference – between As-Is (referring to current strategy and policy) and To-Be. The foundation for the KM strategy is Boh's (2007) Framework of KM-sharing mechanism which takes into account only two determining factors: size and geographical dispersion, and nature of work or problems (see Table 8). Based on these two factors, there are two dimensions, each having two possible and opposing abstract realities (values) resulting in four quadrants of different strategies. The four strategies are individualized-personalization, institutionalized-personalization, individualized-codification, and finally, institutionalized-codification. Put simply, personalization is a People-to-People approach, whereas codification is a People-to-Document approach. The second dimension added by Boh to these two key strategies in the literature contrasts an ad hoc and informal approach (with limited top-down organizational intervention) characterized as 'individualized' with a formal and proactive approach (with planned organizational intervention) characterized as 'institutionalized'. According to the model, personalization or codification depends on the nature of work, being unique or standard, whereas individualized or institutionalized depends on size and geographical dispersion, being small and collocated or large and geographically dispersed. The limitation of this model regarding codification versus personalization is that it does not take into account project amnesia (amplified by personnel turnover) – which may favour codification under any circumstance – and the distinction between the nature of work is a continuum, and in addition, varies within projects taking into account all project activities and related fields. For example, project management is relatively

Table 8 Boh's Mechanisms (Adopted from Boh 2007)

Nature of work or problems	Size and geographical dispersion	
	Small and collocated	Large and geographically dispersed
Unique	Quadrant 1: most suitable for individualized-personalization mechanisms	Quadrant 4: most suitable for institutionalized-personalization mechanisms
Standardized	Quadrant 2: most suitable for individualized-codification mechanisms	Quadrant 3: most suitable for institutionalized-personalization mechanisms

standardized despite tailoring requirements. In contrast, the determining factor for individualized or institutionalized (size and geographical dispersion) is not ambiguous. Arguably, the rationale behind institutionalization is to support knowledge sharing and integration across organizational boundaries (in dispersed organizations, across multiple offices, regions) and across isolated groups of individuals, that is, social networks (in large organizations, often affected by physical boundaries). The alternative, individualized, simply assumes that socialization deals with knowledge processes naturally, ultimately leading to knowledge satisfaction, and that social networks in small and collocated organizations are, per definition, much more integrated. The problem with individualized-codification is that it lacks incentives for knowledge capture. For example, voluntarily writing manuals and procedures are questionable. Also, it could result in duplication. And uncoordinated capture of experience simply will not happen. In most cases, it will be limited to sharing of documents that were once deliverables and are needed as examples. Also, there is no consistent process of knowledge evolution, because knowledge is applied and evaluated in fragmented fashion due to not being available organization wide. ProwLO matches an institutionalized-codification strategy and provides a set of distinct (knowledge sharing) mechanisms as part of an overarching knowledge processing framework, aligned with existing technology. In addition to the above-identified issues around strategy selection, there is also a belief that one strategy should be predominant and the second strategy supportive of the former, and as a rule of thumb, the split should be 80–20 (Hansen et al., 1999).

Links to KM initiatives

The second element includes links to KM initiatives. An overview needs to be provided of all change initiatives related to knowledge management that are planned or were executed in the past. The are two groups of initiatives: technological and organizational, and technological usually have an organizational component. Essentially, these interventions affect knowledge processing by institutionalizing KM mechanisms and technologies in accordance to either personalization or codification. It may be necessary to position these interventions in relation to organizational developments, such as growth, entering new markets, and changes in recruitment policies, indirectly affecting knowledge processes through more fundamental changes in KM infrastructure. One may argue that the individualized strategies lack intervention, and the relevant mechanisms are naturally present, e.g. hallway chats. Some interventions support both codification and personalization. Besides the overview, some concluding remarks can be made on the relation between the KM strategy (ideally) and the portfolio of KM mechanisms and technologies in place or planned for the future, formulated in terms of alignment. This conclusion may be the acknowledgement of alignment of strategy and initiatives or call for new initiatives, such as embedding of ProwLO at organizational level (including implementation of enabling technology), e.g. after initial success of a pilot initiative (managed as project).

ProwLO implementation

The third point addresses implementation of ProwLO. Implementation has two aspects: embedding at organizational level, and adopting the process model at project level. Obviously, there is a dynamic between these two levels. Embedding refers to institutionalization and promotion of ProwLO as an organizational standard. Institutionalization of ProwLO processes, which raises ProwLO practices to routine level, is realized by introduction of supporting software (a key enabler), contributing to process consistency, by ensuring sufficient training, and by designating a change authority for change management, which should be the PMO. Being responsible for change management, the PMO should play a key role in promoting ProwLO as a standard; in the same fashion, it should be responsible for promoting PRINCE2 within an organization. Once ProwLO reaches the status of an organizational standard, institutionalization is further increased by the independent Quality Assurance function and the Project Assurance function at Project Board level (normally an additional responsibility of the Project Board), which checks for adherence to standards in projects. As part of the KM strategy, it is recommended to give a summary (perhaps supported with statistics) on the embedded status of ProwLO, indicated by its actual use in projects, general acknowledgement as best practice, the level of qualification, education and training of key actors, and alignment with other organizational processes (e.g. the presence of PRINCE2 practice).

Adopting ProwLO as part of the project approach is a proposition of the KM strategy that needs Project Board approval, similarly to the rest of the PID. Unlike PRINCE2, ProwLO does not recommend tailoring of its approach (both at organizational and project levels) and there are also no scaling options such as combining roles, combining management products, replacing work flow based on formal documentation with simple communication or format simplification, such as e.g. replacing the PID by a set of presentation slides. The reason is that ProwLO does not conflict with existing practice in any environment, based on any method or approach, and simply has to be aligned with the PRINCE2 process model. The very few alternative Knowledge Management hand-books for project-based organizations, e.g. Knowledge Management for teams and projects (Milton, 2005), may suggest alternative KM techniques but are not capable of replacing ProwLO's process model, the methodology's key asset. The only suggested adaptation is to extend the KM system in scope-covering projects, CoP and centres of excellence in order to perfect knowledge processing or increase learning capability of individuals and groups. In extending the scope of the KM system it is important to consider the social dimension of knowledge. So additional mechanisms, methods and techniques should take into account a People and Culture dimen-sion, besides IT alignment.

Furthermore, only the PRINCE2 generic processes and specific interfaces are essential, so it matters that any tailored PRINCE2 appli-cation satisfies the requirements that follows: an overarching frame-work for parallel PKM processes aligned with PRINCE2 at a high level, and common interfaces for interaction between the two meth-odologies. So, the decision to adopt ProwLO is a fundamental one. The recommendation is that if institutionalized-codification is part of the strategy, then every single project should use ProwLO (exceptions aside).

Unlike PRINCE2, which has to deal with bureaucratic overload for small projects, the overhead due to ProwLO is highly flexible and depends on the volume of unsatisfied project and organizational knowledge needs, leading to knowledge activities and additional coordination requirements, and, furthermore, the necessity of pro-active problem solving supported by knowledge capture and enabled by case-based reasoning. In other words, overhead is a variable with flexible work load. It cannot be ignored, however, that some projects are more important than others in a portfolio (based on criteria like size and strategic importance), and also in terms of knowledge gains. Consequently, this may have impact on specific ProwLO processes (e.g. by omitting certain activities, not to be confused with tailoring), or even result in not adopting ProwLO at all (and thus, making an exception), based on the assumption that the overhead would not weigh against the expected benefits. It should be stressed, however, that not all benefits relate to *new* knowledge gains and captured knowledge. Other benefits include the prominence of knowledge needs satisfaction as a guiding principle, and the acknowledgement of the key role of knowledge reuse – of organizational knowledge – in satisfying those needs. In practice, an additional complication could be limited resources with regard to availability of skilled project knowledge managers. As a consequence, no person might be able to fulfil the role of project knowledge manager in a given project as part of the project team, and thus, ProwLO might simply be infeasible. In addition to the proposition of adopting ProwLO for the current project, general and project-specific arguments may be provided. Examples of project-specific arguments are a pilot project mandate and project interfaces with particular projects depending on knowledge transfer (e.g. as part of a larger programme). This involves a short analysis of benefits (including abstract ones as mentioned above) and specific business triggers relating to current organizational problems. Awareness of business problems with a KM component is important for overall commitment to knowledge management practice. In some cases, the project knowledge manager may refer to the project mandate at corporate or programme level, first used in Staring Up a Project, that provides a clear instruction to apply ProwLO.

Knowledge strategy process

The fourth and final point of the KM strategy is to address links with a Knowledge Strategy Process (KSP). The KSP, as introduced by Hofer-Alfeis and van der Spek (2002), is a method that explicitly addresses knowledge areas, which call for differentiated actions for their further development in terms of proficiency, diffusion and codification, as each knowledge area scores differently As-Is and To-Be according to these three dimensions. Taking into account the organizational scope, proficiency is most likely an average based on the skills of all people involved, and diffusion is probably the degree that all that is known (and quantifiable as explicit knowledge or inferable as tacit knowledge) by individuals is shared organization wide (it relates to inequality in knowledge possession and knowledge fragmentation across individuals). Within knowledge areas, there could be huge fluctuations at knowledge entity level which complicates the overall picture (objectively, diffusion is the average commonness of knowledge and corresponding overall variance (relating to distribution differences within a knowledge area and adding to fragmentation instead of diffusion) in a given population). Codification is a proportional measure comparing captured knowledge (embedded in artefacts) with the estimated total amount of tacit knowledge represented by individuals and/or uncodified explicit knowledge that surfaces in the act of knowing (i.e. application) and dynamics of knowledge conversion but is not prepared for knowledge retention. It should be noted that assigning scores to knowledge areas according this method, e.g. based on Likert scales, is not a math exercise but involves expert judgement. Fortunately, this is a team exercise (see below). Besides the focus on knowledge areas, the KSP also provides a business perspective by capturing the business context that determines the direction of the knowledge strategy (this ensures alignment) and identifies key performance indicators derived from the business strategy (e.g. based on the balanced scorecard). Based on this information, it is possible to estimate the impact (using a Likert-scale) of the various knowledge areas on business performance *as a whole* taking into account these key performance indicators.

The KSP is performed by the business owners and their management team and consists of six steps. The first step is to define the business case. In project management terms, it provides the reason for initiating a project. In this context, the business case depicts a vision of the business for the near future, supported by strategy and planning, which may or may not call for business transformation and pragmatic actions targeting development of knowledge areas supporting that vision. The business case takes into account major organizational changes (e.g. launch of a new product line) and major trends in the environment underlying many changes.

The second step is to determine which knowledge areas are significant in the context of the business case, including those knowledge areas that are essential to current business operations. Hofer-Alfeis & van der Spek define a knowledge area as 'thematic consolidation of experiences, theories, finding and abilities in the various manifestation of the knowledge model' (referring to their three dimensions of knowledge). In simple terms, knowledge areas are knowledge groups based on a shared theme. Unlike ProwLO, the KSP does not make a distinction between knowledge domains and areas, as introduced in 'Introduce Knowledge Processes' for the purpose of metadata. Also, it does not provide any reference in defining knowledge areas, other than a direct link with business challenges and dominant business operations. Based on their examples, it follows that knowledge areas are rooted in business concerns; for example, whether a company has the know-how to develop energy-saving engines; and whether there is enough available expertise to conclude projects successfully. The first example refers to new technology and the second

example refers to project management, and both are eligible knowledge areas, although both can be split based on subthemes. KSP
acknowledges a need for methods to identify and structure knowledge areas, but recommends to make a list of 10–12 knowledge
areas in total. Taking into account subthemes and their potential
diversity in terms of proficiency, diffusion and codification, this recommendation may be too limited. It could be interesting for some
knowledge areas to unravel sub-themes for a more accurate and
diverse view.

The third step is to list all relevant key performance indicators
(KPIs) based on the business case in step 1. This step can be alter-
nated with step 2. The source of these indicators should be an explicit business strategy. Usually, an organization adopts KPIs after
defining organizational goals in order to measure performance and
progress.

In step 4, all knowledge areas are assessed on their current and
future impact on *each* key performance indicator. The outcome of
this analysis is a so-called 'knowledge portfolio' in which knowledge
areas are 'subjected to a two-dimensional weighting'. This involves
segregating knowledge areas into four groups (i.e. quadrants) based
on their degree of impact currently and in the future, using a Likert
scale. These groups are not relevant, basic, promising and key. See
Figure 9 for an illustration.

Step 5 involves assessment of the status of knowledge areas in
terms of proficiency, dissemination and codification, in particular of
those areas that score higher in the knowledge portfolio of the previous step. The assessment results in a Knowledge Status Guide help to
determine in which areas the organization should improve. Diffusion
is represented by the x-axis, while Codification is represented by the
y-axis. Each knowledge area in the status chart has a beginning point,
corresponding to the current status, and an end point, corresponding
to the target status, and the two are connected with a line. The third
dimension of proficiency is represented by a number before and
after the knowledge area label next to the line. The lines in the chart
indicate how much change is required, and together with the knowledge portfolio, the knowledge status guide provides a foundation for
the proposition of knowledge management actions, targeting specific
knowledge areas. Figure 10 provides an illustration.

The final step, step 6, consists of three sub-activities. In the first
sub-activity, the management team proposes actions in alignment
with the business strategy and their understanding of the knowledge
areas. For large and important areas, it may be necessary to run

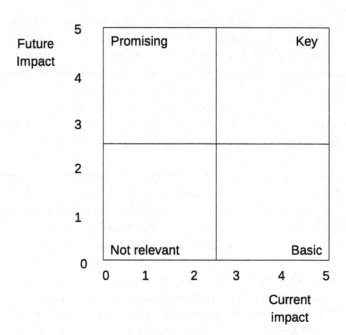

Figure 9 Knowledge Portfolio.

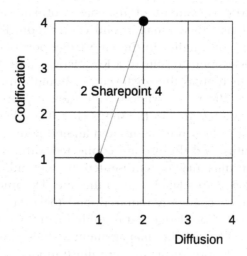

Figure 10 Knowledge Status Guide.

additional knowledge strategy processes (based on sub-themes). Most likely, these analyses will require involvement of management and specialists as subject-experts, and can be facilitated with workshops. Hence, the KSP is potentially an iterative process. The second sub-step takes place after any detailed workshops and focuses on the integration of actions. This entails grouping actions into cross-knowledge area and area-specific. Second, the actions are rated in the overall KSP context for prioritization purposes. The final sub-activity concerns with design and planning of solutions strategies. Essentially, this may trigger implementation of state-of-the art solutions, including enabling technologies. From an organizational point of view, this is critical because knowledge managers, including the Chief Knowledge Officer (if applicable), often lack the authority to enforce fundamental changes and business transformations. In practice, often, manager's support for KM projects is lacking and this approach solves this. For a long list of sample knowledge management actions, see Hofer-Alfeis and van der Spek (2002), which were derived from their case study. It is highly recommendable to hire external KM consultants to facilitate the KSP.

The KSP nicely fits with ProwLO. It acknowledges the importance of diffusion, and thus knowledge integration in general as part of the knowledge value chain, and codification, deliberate knowledge capture, which precedes dissemination of explicit knowledge, also part of the knowledge value chain. In addition, the proficiency dimension of knowledge, which is always tied to people based on their skills and abilities, is another aspect which greatly contributes to the success of a business. Proficiency not only depends on attracting the right people with the right qualifications but also on experience accumulation, i.e. learning on the job but also on being able to rely on the experience of others, who may or may not be on the same project, and continuous learning in general. So, to a certain degree, proficiency relies on project memory based on experiences such as lessons learned and cases, and thus, calls for their knowledge capture. Furthermore, the knowledge areas identified in the process together with their actual and target status in all three dimensions provide an incentive in projects to focus on organizational knowledge needs related to these areas. In particular, the priority given to specific areas can be used as a theme-based directive for knowledge capture as part of the Live capture process. In other words, the KSP may drive knowledge capture. Other knowledge processes in projects may also be affected. So, in the context of the project KM strategy, a statement may be provided on the impact of the KSP on project-specific knowledge processes covering specific knowledge areas and underlying *organizational* knowledge needs in the light of closing knowledge and experience gaps across the organization.

In principle, the project KM strategy adopted should be aligned with the corporate KM strategy, which in turn should be aligned with the business strategy and Information Tecnology (IT) strategy (as KM may have an IT component, and usually has). To align the business strategy with the IT strategy is a challenge on its own. Venkatraman (1993) provides four dominant alignment perspectives taking into account, on the one hand, external orientation (characteristic for strategy) and internal orientation (characteristic for infrastructure and processes), and on the other hand, both domains (business and IT). Each perspective is driven by the business strategy or the IT strategy and has distinct management implications.

The corporate KM strategy may have a unique format, if documented, but should cover the four elements of the project KM strategy: Boh's fundamental strategies, KM initiatives, ProwLO and outcomes of Knowledge Strategy Processes, as these elements have generic qualities, applying to a portfolio of projects. The KSP in particular is an extension of corporate strategy-bound constraints and directives. Hence, ideally, the project KM strategy should resemble the corporate KM strategy. But, at the same time, it should be possible to challenge basic assumptions set forth at corporate level based on new insight and emerging project needs. This raises the need for an interface and evaluation of KM strategy based on feedback from actual projects.

SET UP KNOWLEDGE MANAGEMENT SYSTEM

The term Knowledge Management System is ambiguous. It can either refer to a combination of KM mechanisms and technologies, that complement each other and potentially interact, or a tool, IT system. ProwLO adopts the former interpretation based on Becerra's model of KM Solutions (see Figure 11). According to this model, KM systems are the integration of technologies and mechanisms that are developed to support KM processes. KM mechanisms are organizational (or structural) means to promote KM processes, while KM technologies involve the use of IT. KM mechanisms include well-defined methods and more abstract approaches. A Project Knowledge Portal is an example of a technology and

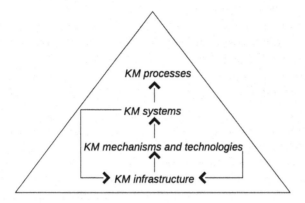

Figure 11 Conceptual Model of KM Solutions.

a tool. Unlike Becerra proposes, no distinction is made between categories of KM systems based on the specific knowledge processes they intently support. She distinguishes knowledge discovery systems, knowledge capture systems, knowledge sharing systems and knowledge application systems. The main reason is that a KM system can be regarded as the complete portfolio of KM mechanisms and technologies in an organization, which by nature should complement one another. The other reason is that even if you zoom in at sub-system level, you may find that some individual technologies and mechanisms cluster – evidenced by process integration – to form a coherent solution, and thereby support multiple knowledge processes. As long as additional technologies and mechanism can be complemented in a narrow sense or integrated with this tool, it is difficult to speak in terms of distinct KM systems. Also, new functionality added to IT systems can expand their scope in terms of knowledge process support.

Setting of a KM system is essentially establishing the portfolio of KM mechanisms and technologies based on an overall conception of the desired KM system, in alignment with the KM strategy. The starting point is the conceptual knowledge needs (i.e. knowledge types) that need to be addressed by the system. Instead of using the complete list of distinguishable knowledge types, as provided in section 'Reusable Project Knowledge' in Chapter 1, it is recommendable to make a selection based on priority. In some cases, the proposed mechanisms and technologies may support multiple types, including ones that are not listed. The next step is to link the selected knowledge types with knowledge processes based on the PKVC. Knowledge types are essentially managed by knowledge processes. After this step, specific KM mechanism and technologies are proposed to support individual knowledge processes related to specific knowledge types. Overall, this mapping represents a proposition (to-be). The focus on specific knowledge types and knowledge processes is driven by the business case, comparable with the KSP. This may limit the scope of the KM system. Accordingly, there could be other potential KM technologies and mechanisms that may add up to the total portfolio and organizational KM system as a whole. The final step is to describe the current organizational status regarding each single KM technology and mechanism, namely regarding its use or current limitations. This allows to compare the current situation with the ideal situation. Similar to the project KM strategy, there should be an interface for feedback processes with authorities that are responsible for implementation and maintenance of KM systems, most likely the same people responsible for corporate KM strategy. The presence of such interfaces contributes to the overall dynamic capability of organizations, a notion popularized by Peter Senge and key foundation of his 'Learning Organization'.

In Appendix I, there are two examples in table format of the proposed KM systems, including an analysis of the current situation. Both case studies were performed at different international engineering consulting companies, both first established in the Netherlands. Nearly all of the proposed KM technologies and mechanisms found in the two tables will be elaborated in further detail as they form part of the backbone of ProwLO. The exceptions are Management Information System (MIS) and Expertise Centre. A Management Information System, sometimes called quality management system (in conformance to a quality standard), is normally a web-based intranet solution supporting the knowledge needs of mainly project managers. One of the cases is ARCADIS, whose MIS contains a process model (based on the in-house methodology discussed in Chapter 2), process descriptions and various documents related to specific processes (templates, guidelines, checklists, instructions, etc.). As such, an MIS takes full advantage of the web-based paradigm, which is acknowledged as a distinct KM technology. However, the orientation of an MIS is limited since it focuses on project methodologies, limiting support for various knowledge types (e.g. Cases and Lessons Learned). In this light, a Project Knowledge Portal is regarded as an enhanced information system compared to an MIS capable of dealing with a vast array of different types of knowledge objects with better lifecycle support (just think of the Project Knowledge Value Chain embedded in the software). Although an MIS fosters compliance to corporate standards such as project methodologies (thus also supporting knowledge application), it has little complementary value to a Project Knowledge Portal because the latter has the capability to embed project methodologies (very simply by copying the whole concept or more advanced integration like, for example, workflow support). However, if an MIS is currently present in an organization, this should not be neglected and addressed in the table to put things in perspective. The Expertise Centre is essentially an evolved Project Management Office able to support project team members based on their needs; it is very useful, but not essential for ProwLO.

Looking at the tables in Appendix I, note that the role of PRINCE2 is included as part of the solution. Some PRINCE2 activities and management products can be directly linked to knowledge processes or KM mechanisms, not KM technologies as PRINCE2 is intentionally technology neutral. Also, note the inclusion of 'Project-based learning' (PBL). PBL relates to experience accumulation and is a manifestation of knowledge production. In principle, it is desirable that the KM system should support PBL to any possible degree. Note that Alerts in case 2 are replaced by IntraKnotes in case 1. Finally, Project Knowledge Portal technology provides the same support as the fundamental web-based access in the context of knowledge integration.

A lot of knowledge types can be represented by container knowledge objects and digitally distributed as document files. Accordingly, one may regard such knowledge objects, derived from different knowledge types, as Tools supporting various project processes. This approach to Tools as an umbrella concept makes sense in the context of knowledge processes because many knowledge types can be processed (from knowledge creation to knowledge evolution) similarly despite their intrinsic differences. The determining factor here is format, knowing that documents can be used as carriers of knowledge, same as people. The benefit is that in setting up the KM system, the project knowledge manager does not have to consider each and every knowledge type individually, resulting in better table oversight and less redundancy.

The KM mechanisms and KM technologies as part of the proposed KM system highlighted in both tables, closely aligned with ProwLO, will be discussed in the following sections and are grouped based on the specific knowledge process they *primarily* support. For each process, the role of PRINCE2 will also be discussed.

KNOWLEDGE CAPTURE

Project reviews

Project reviews are a key KM mechanism for knowledge capture in projects. Project reviews are also quite common in many types of organizations, across industries, but in most cases not obligatory (or, as in ARCADIS, only obligatory for projects with a certain amount of budget) and often executed poorly, for example, due to time pressure. Based on timing, three types of project reviews can be distinguished: project reviews during the project, at the end of a project, or at some moment in time after a project has ended ('Project Post-Mortem'). ProwLO acknowledges both the importance of post-control methods for the end of project review and Gate-reviews during the project. As any method, this should include process-based characteristics as well as documentation aspects, i.e. guidance on type of content to be captured. In contrary, Schindler and Eppler's (2003) interpretation makes a distinction between process-based methods (such as project reviews) and document-based methods (such as learning histories), failing to see that each method process – sequential, event- and/or time-driven, and carried out based on the presumption of similar circumstances – has an output perspective (as made explicit in process-data diagrams); most likely their interpretation is helped by the fact that some notions lack associated format, while other notions lack process context.

ProwLO would like to challenge organizations to develop a project review method (or methods) based on their organizational experience, taking into account different timing for postcontrol and gate reviews. With regard to content-based requirements, the method should acknowledge at least Cases and Lessons Learned. And with regard to process-based requirements – in this case following content requirements, both postcontrol and gate reviews should take into account the Cases-method (introduced below), safeguarded by ProwLO. A key aspect is to facilitate meetings in which the project teams come together, which may require a common format and could be based on best practices. It should be noted that project reviews are similar to a 'project audit'. The main difference is that in the latter case, reviews are carried out by project-external people, either some quality assurance function or external audit firm.

Gate reviews are founded upon transitions from one individual project phase to another. They are called gate reviews because of the underlying stage-gate paradigm (von Zedtwitz, 2002) inherent to

PRINCE2, which is materialized through key decision moments dividing projects into Stages. The stage-gate development process of projects offers a particularly good framework for learning opportunities (Loch & Morris, 2003). As compared to postcontrol, there is less risk of project amnesia. Also, gate reviews complement postcontrol in the sense that they may enhance project-based learning *during* the project with positive project impact, while the project still can be influenced. The advantage of postcontrol is that a complete picture of project behaviour can be constructed reflecting all events, which enables better understanding and thus more sound knowledge claims. Therefore, ProwLO suggests a combination of these two types of project reviews, in which postcontrol can be used to refine and consolidate captured knowledge during gate reviews. Note in the section about the role of PRINCE2 in relation to knowledge capture that similar progression can be observed from the use of the Lessons Learned Log and Lessons Learned Report, which can be associated with the proposed KM mechanisms for knowledge capture. Also, the mechanism of Live Capture (see below) may benefit from the use of the Lessons Learned Log. However, postcontrol and gate reviews involve more complexity as to be regarded timing-based activities for just maintaining two container documents based on a standard template. Moreover, Lessons Learned is one of many knowledge types worthwhile noting. For a starter, the Lessons Learned Log and Report should be expanded with Cases by incorporating the associated standard format into the overall template. This format is based on the Cases-method introduced below and added as Appendix III.

The project post-mortems are especially useful for projects in which the benefits need to be evaluated/valued in the future, as some effects may need time for business impact and accurate measurement, long after a project finishes. For instance, Post-Project Appraisal (PPA), which is a method published by Frank A. Gulliver, is conducted approximately two years after project completion (in Schindler & Eppler, 2003). However, from the viewpoint of knowledge management, project post-mortems are less interesting as after a long period of time, a significant amount of project memory will become irreversibly fragmented due to project amnesia (i.e. 'lost for good').

Project Reviews are generally part of Project Evaluation, a subfunction of Project Management and at the same time a key focus area of Project Knowledge Management (PKM). This raises the question again whether PKM is a component of PM. Although PM methodologies and other bodies of knowledge provide some guidance on project evaluation, they are limited in know-how and do not address

knowledge management problems in project-driven organizations suffi-
ciently nor elaborate on the notion of learning. ProwLO was designed
to complement, not compete, with PM methodologies in this respect. In
practice, evaluation is sometimes devaluated by a narrow focus on project performance, at the expense of learning in general in all its variety.
ProwLO counters this tendency by raising awareness of the organizational impact of project-based learning and knowledge capture.

Live capture

The limitation of pre-determined time-bands associated with postcontrol and gate reviews is that they do not necessarily correspond with
learning needs. Anecdotal evidence can be found in empirical
research by Newell et al. (2004) on sharing learning across projects,
in which an interviewee stated that, 'Personally I think that is the best
time to learn – when you have to'. This is further supported by quantitative research by Fong and Yip (2006) who conclude that when pro-
fessionals discover meaningful lessons, they should record them
immediately. Hence, ProwLO is also an advocate of live capture.

Without a real business trigger, live capture will never have a chance to
become a routine. Spontaneous behaviour is definitely not a reliable process and, without encouragement, it will not be repeated. A specific problem that emerges with live capture is that it takes time and resources for
learning and knowledge capture. Unlike planned approaches before-
hand, it may be difficult to reserve time and allocate necessary resources
(for reflection, discussion, documentation, etc.) in ad hoc fashion such
as live capture, especially because learning associated with knowledge
gaining is often difficult to predict. Paradoxically, a policy promoting
live capture may inhibit project-based learning, if not compensated by
additional formal project reviews. This is due to the fact that in cases
where project members experience a high level of time pressure, learning could be perceived as conflicting with the short-term goals of a project, which, generally speaking, can be defined as how to get from State
A to State B quickly, cheaply and effectively (Barnes, 2002). ProwLO
deals with this issue in two ways. First, by incorporating the 'After Action
Review' (AAR) method as part of the overall Live Capture process (see
Chapter 7). Performing this method may trigger (live) capture of Cases.
And, second, by copying the PRINCE2 activity of Examining Issues and
Risk, now performed by the Project Knowledge Manager, which may
trigger escalation of Issues and Risks, and which in turn may result in
the capture of Cases also (and live). In any case, Live capture requires
a pro-active attitude towards learning. Note that gate reviews may

validate knowledge that was captured live, in a similar fashion that postcontrol complements gate reviews.

AAR helps to learn immediately from errors and successes, regardless of the length of the task in question (Collinson, 2005). In other words, the AAR does not have to be performed at the end of a project or activity. Rather, it can be performed after each identifiable event within a project or major activity, thus becoming a live learning process (Clark, 2004). AAR was originally developed by the US army for soldiers in crisis periods during and after missions, where a complete evaluation is not possible (Schindler & Eppler, 2003). There are various formats, ranging from 20-min brainstorming to 2-hour discussion sessions. In an AAR, a team is confronted with four main questions, namely (Schindler & Eppler, 2003):

- What was supposed to happen?
- What actually happened?
- Why were the differences?
- What can you learn from this experience?

The learning points are captured on a flip chart, which is referred to on relevant occasions, e.g. before or during similar situations.

There is a strong connection between AAR and the concept of 'Cases' as both deal with problem situations. The last mechanism for knowledge capture that will be introduced below, namely the Cases-method, could be considered as an extension of AAR, specifically addressing the content that should be captured concerning Cases.

Cases-method

The Cases-method is a proprietary method open for licensing. This method was constructed as a procedure to capture Cases, problem+solution scenarios, including the Lessons Learned that could be derived from them. The same technique, process deliverable/data diagrams, was used for this method as for ProwLO processes. Figure 12 provides a graphical overview of the method.

Background

Before giving a step-by-step explanation, some remarks should be given about the background of the method. The method is meant to demonstrate the results of particular *management* actions, which provide lessons for future projects. Accordingly, the scope of the method is limited to

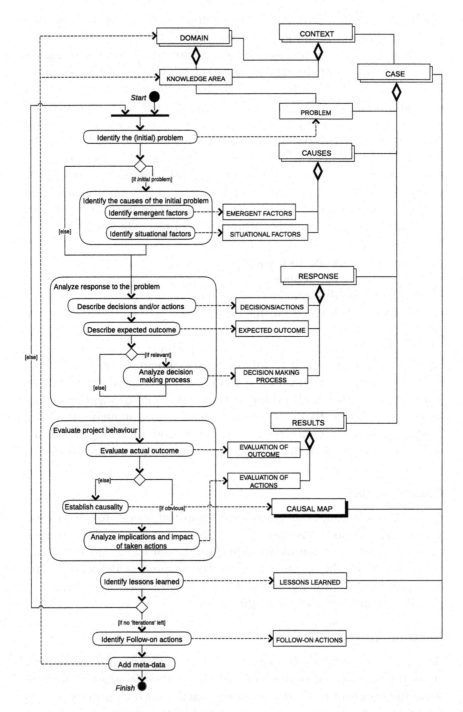

Figure 12 Cases-Method.

the project management domain. However, the problem-solving paradigm based on causal reasoning is quite universal. So applying this method to specialist, technical domains may require only slight changes. Some of the fundamentals of the method were derived – by means of abstraction – from a case example and its corresponding causal structure (see Williams, 2003, p. 448 or Appendix II). Furthermore, it addresses easy lessons learned as well as hard lessons from projects (Williams, 2004). Easy lessons are those lessons that can be articulated readily or without too much difficulty. Hard lessons, on the other hand, are much harder to explicate. In both cases, lessons typically include *know-why* (i.e. insights into cause–effect relationships) and some *know-how* (e.g. procedural or heuristic knowledge). The difference, however, resides in the complexity of the know-why. If the implications and impact of taken actions are obvious, then it is assumed that lessons can be readily articulated as well. So here we are dealing with easy lessons. If, however, they are not, implying that lessons are non-obvious as well, then causality should be established first. The latter involves externalization of tacit knowledge (know-why) but may also lead to knowledge discovery (note extra learning), especially in case of limited understanding prior to defining a causal model.

As management actions often set up feedback loops that drive project behaviour, it is often difficult to analyze (project) behaviour in terms of causality. Feedback refers to the self-correcting or self-reinforcing side effects of decisions (Sterman, 1992, p. 7). For example, when a project falls behind schedule, one possible managerial response is the use of overtime. The extra hours help bring the project back on schedule, reducing the need for overtime in the future. Such a feedback process is self-correcting. However, if overtime remains high for an extended period, workers may become fatigued and burned out, leading to lower productivity, a higher rate of errors and increased employee turnover, thus further delaying the project and leading to pressure for still more overtime, in a vicious cycle or self-reinforcing feedback process (Sterman, 1992, p. 7). Feedback processes may result in non- or counter-intuitive behaviour in projects, such as, for example, 'we doubled our workforce on this project but it yielded only 5% extra output' (Williams, 2004). According to Williams (2003), many (potential) lessons cannot be identified by unaided reflection, particularly due to feedback structures within projects. These vicious cycles which are formed and which contribute to the cost of disruption and delay normally centre around two issues: productivity losses and the rework cycle (Eden et al., 2000).

Following Williams (2003), it is suggested to make use of a modelling technique to create cause-maps and to identify feedback processes. It should be noted that this type of analysis, concerning the hard lessons from projects, is not worthwhile in every type of projects.

According to Williams (2004), it becomes worthwhile for projects:

- that are complex,
- where few or no managers have an overview of the whole project,
- where there is the potential for delay/disruption type of effects, in particular where there is a customer involved; customers in design-intensive projects can cause significant problems which set up heavy feedback loops; or in retrospect,
- which are highly time-constrained so heavy acceleration has been needed,
- where quantitative out-turns have been unexpected and intuitively difficult to understand.

Step-by-step explanation

The first step is to identify the initial problem. For example, common problems in (engineering) projects are project variations (i.e. deviations from plan), such as significant schedule and cost overrun.

Next, one has to identify the causes behind the problem. Usually, this involves a combination of emergent factors (unpredicted events) and situational factors (specific circumstances).

The third step is to analyze the management actions. The output is a description of the corrective action(s) and expected outcome. Optionally, some notes can be made on the decision-making process. Whether this information is considered as 'relevant' may depend on the nature of the decision-making process. For instance, in case of rational decision-making, the decision-making process basically consists of problem recognition, formulation of alternative courses of action(s) and selection of an alternative that accomplishes the predefined goal (Joshi, 2001). One can imagine that capturing this kind of knowledge is valuable for learning purposes. However, in case decision-making is rather political and controlled through power and influence, obviously, the matter becomes more complicated. Even if the decision-making process can be characterized as rational, one should be aware that managers (as any human being) have a bounded rationality. So, for instance, the amount of information a manager had upon which to base decision should not be overestimated (hindsight). It may be in the interest of the project manager to stress this out so that he or she could be held less accountable for certain project outcomes. The project manager may also wish to note that a particular decision involved an 'instinctive' gut-feel (Williams, 2004). Furthermore, managers may express their satisfaction with regard to the process (including the role of the project board). Relevant questions in this respect may include: was there lack of information, communication, expertise, capacity, support, etc.? Of course, this requires a culture of openness.

The next step is to evaluate the project behaviour. This evaluation addresses the actual outcome, for example, in terms of adjustment of contract duration, total direct and indirect cost, or both, and includes an analysis of the consequences (implications) and impact of the taken actions that (may) have affected that outcome. If the implications and impact are not obvious, then causality should be established first by the means of modelling (in order to capture feedback loops). Subsequently, one should draw lessons learned.

It should be stressed that managerial events are often repetitive cycles of decision–implementation–feedback–decision. New iterations may start when the initial problem has not been solved (or only partly) or when a new problem has arisen due to project behaviour. In case the initial problem persists, there is usually no need to identify additional emergent and situational factors, unless some factors have been neglected or new emergent factors obstructed effectiveness of taken decision and actions in the course of time. Alternatively, a new problem may arise, not necessarily a new Case (!) – fragmentation of problems may not be desirable. The new problem is usually caused by project behaviour from the previous iteration. Despite the newness of the problem, emergent and situational factors usually correspond to the causes of the previous problem. In short, identification of situational and emergent factors is mandatorily the first iteration (as depicted in the process-data model above), but may be readdressed in subsequent iterations, if only for refinement purposes. If there are no more iterations left, as witnessed by project behaviour and lack of new events with Case impact, and realized in retrospect (by the decision-maker or observer), the next step is to add follow-up actions. Follow-up actions may effectuate Lessons Learned, leading, for example, to changes in organizational routines.

The last step is to add 'meta-data' to the Case such as e.g. domain (in our case, Project Management) and related knowledge area(s) (which can be multiple). The concept of domain can be defined as an overarching concept (e.g. a paradigm or practice) consisting of several knowledge areas (or sub-domains).

The closest alternative is Toyata's A3 approach for structured problem solving and continuous improvement. A3 is also known as SPS ('Systemic Problem Solving') as stated in Wikipedia (last checked on

9 February 2018). One of the key differences is that the Cases-method stresses the iterative nature of decision-making and project behaviour. The A3 method also does not address meta-data, etc.

Role of PRINCE2

PRINCE2 prescribes several activities that involve the use of an Issue Log, Risk Log, Lessons Learned Log and Lessons Learned Report. The Issue Log contains a list of all project issues, including deviations such as 'Requests for Change' and 'Off-specifications'. Regarding each issue, there is a description of the issue, how it is assessed, what decisions were made and the current status. The Issue Log often lies at the root of valuable knowledge. The results of a risk analysis are maintained in the Risk Log. Risk Management is a continuous process as new information becomes available and circumstances change as the project progresses. In practice, risks are usually being evaluated at the end of each Stage or as part of a situation that involves an Exception. Risks are potential problem situations. If risks are perceived as unacceptable, then the project manager has to anticipate and take countermeasures. The latter is essentially a case of acting upon a problem. Hence, risks may eventually result in management Cases. The Lessons Learned Log is used for maintaining Lesson Learned during the project, whereas the Lessons Learned Report adds to, consolidates and corrects information contained in the Lessons Learned Log in the context of Closing a Project, when the activity 'Evaluate Project' is triggered.

When we take a closer look at the management of deviations in projects, it can be found that PRINCE2 offers control based on capture of management information, explained below. In addition, ProwLO acknowledges the importance of such management information in the context of the capture of Cases. The general PRINCE2 process states that the examination of deviations, including their causes and effects, may lead to corrective actions and/or changes in the Stage or Project Plan. If the deviation from the planning (with all its implications) is problematic but does not exceed one or more tolerances (with regard to scope, benefits, quality, risk, time and/or costs), the project manager may initiate corrective actions by himself/herself – with or without ad hoc support from the Project Board. If, however, one or more tolerances are exceeded (or as expected) due to project behaviour (without or despite corrective actions), then these issues are the so-called 'Exceptions' and have to be discussed with the Project Board first. It should be stressed that tolerances not only apply to the deviation itself but also to corrective actions. To facilitate discussion and increase control, an Exception Report is written by the project manager and provided to the Project Board. Subsequently, based on feedback from the Board, an Exception Plan is created. It should be noted that this exception procedure is based on the principle of management-by-exception. The motives for an Exception may be rooted in (Onna & Koning, 2002):

- Insufficient human effort.
- Too high costs.
- A change request with a high impact on the Stage or Project Plan.
- A delivered product that does not conform the Product Description (Off-specification) and cannot be fixed within the tolerances.
- Assumptions in the Business Case do not hold in reality, and thus, the project cannot be justified any longer.
- A foreseen risk that becomes reality.
- An unforeseen risk that has been identified.

Guided by agreed tolerances within the framework of Project Planning, deviations leading to Corrective actions or Exceptions resulting in either approval of corrective actions or Exception Plans are perfect management examples suitable for capture as Cases, provided that this type of capture addresses knowledge needs.

The fact that PRINCE2 provides management concepts relevant to knowledge capture makes it interesting to look at PRINCE2 activities dealing with these concepts, that is, management products. Accordingly, PRINCE2 enforces elements of the ProwLO process model, which relies on consistent use of these products. Table 2 provides an overview:

Table 9 PRINCE2 and Knowledge Capture

Activity	Products
Setting Up Project Files (IP5)	Issue Log, Lessons Learned Log (amongst others)
Capturing (CS3) & Examining Project Issues (CS4)	Issue Log
Updating the Risk Log (SB4) *and Lessons Learned Log*	Risk Log, Lessons Learned Log
Decommissioning a Project (CP1)	Issue Log
Evaluating a Project (CP3)	Lessons Learned Report
Confirming Project Closure (DP5)	Lessons Learned Report

None of the above activities are conflicting or redundant with
ProwLO. They complement. Capture and examine issues and risks
in ProwLO is an additional activity carried out by the Project Knowledge Manager. However, PRINCE2 fails to address that some of
the sub-activities involved can be performed by roles other than
the Project Manager. The argument for delegating part of the associated capture (in this case, management information or knowledge, or ambiguous) is to lessen the burden on the Project
Manager. Being responsible for the Issue Log, Risk Log, Lessons
Learned Log *and* Lessons Learned Report simply could be too
much work for the project manager, Since all of the above activities initially deal with project management information, it follows
that capture is here a project support function, if delegated. In
ProwLO, this type of project support should be performed by the
Project Knowledge Manager. Hence, the scope of ProwLO may be
extended to extra project management activities as defined in
PRINCE2, or potentially any other PM methodology which applies
similar management concepts. Taking the role of the Project Manager as the starting point (in a PRINCE2 environment), and assuming
that the Risk Log is maintained by a specialist Risk Manager, there are
three possible options:

- The Project Manager only uses the Issue Log.
- The Project Manager uses the Issue Log and is responsible for the
  Lessons Learned Log, implying he/she has a leading role in
  knowledge capture, potentially also at the level of directing knowledge capture (the responsibility of the Project Knowledge Manager in ProwLO).
- The Project Manager uses the Issue Log and is responsible for
  Lessons Learned and Lessons Learned Report, adding significant knowledge management responsibilities at the end of
  a project.

Each of these three options has impact on the role of the Project
Knowledge Manager acting as project support. And the combined
responsibilities of both Project Manager and Project Knowledge Manager, divided between them, have unique advantages and disadvantages. For example, a dominant role of the Project Manager has the
advantage (from his/her point of view – which is to be respected) of
having more autonomy and influence in directing knowledge capture
(allowing defensive behaviour due to accountability in case of negative experience). The disadvantages are more tasks for the PM, less

direction by the Project Knowledge Manager, and uncertain quality and consistency of Cases and Lessons Learned. Consequently, if a Project Knowledge Manager is acknowledged – beyond the notion of conventional project support – the process of project knowledge management will likely suffer from overlapping responsibility. Generally, greater responsibility of the Project Manager in knowledge capture comes at the expense of social learning processes (less facilitated meetings, less interviewing opportunities for the Project Knowledge Manager as a means to elicit knowledge, etc.), and also poses that the PM has the necessary skills to perform knowledge capture in a rather self-reliant way (e.g. being able to apply the Cases-method in an adequate manner).

ProwLO propagates that the Project Manager should only use the Issue Log (!), and thus, the Project Knowledge Manager should be aware of and able to execute specific tasks in the context of some PRINCE2 activities. As such, Project Knowledge Management shows overlap with Project Management, or, actually, knowledge management practices are embedded in a project management methodology. In Company Y, one of the participants in the case study noted that this option is too demanding for project support as part of the Project Support Office (better known as Project Management Office). However, the distinct role of a Project Knowledge Manager, who specializes in knowledge capture, was not addressed back then. Another participant, on the other hand, believed it is the best option in spite of her interpretation of project support, based on the perception that project managers are too busy anyway – in support of the argument for delegation. A deciding factor that became apparent in the case study, namely project size (placing more burden on the Project Manager and increasing the need for project support), is irrelevant in the context of ProwLO, which does not need scaling (see section 'Prepare KM Strategy', sub-section 'ProwLO Implementation'). A specific problem in conventional project management is that project support cannot rely on an Issue Log alone for the delivery of the Lessons Learned Log and Lessons Learned Report, due to overall passivity in the knowledge management process or lack of project commitment. In any case, in alignment with the earlier proposed KM mechanisms for knowledge capture, all three management products are required for effective application of ProwLO. Omitting one of these mechanisms seriously compromises ProwLO and may result in inconformity to PRINCE2's use of the aforementioned management products.

KNOWLEDGE INTEGRATION

Web-based access

Web-based access applies to all conceptual knowledge needs eligible for knowledge reuse. This single fact makes this technology a central component of the proposed KM system, a key enabler of organizational learning. Obviously, organizational learning is a function of the level of knowledge integration, aside from actual knowledge application (reuse), especially when it triggers more profound project evaluation (following personal internalization) with social feedback. Naturally, the responsibility for integrating knowledge via web-based access belongs to the Project Knowledge Manager as part of Content Management, which is incorporated into ProwLO. Effective and efficient knowledge integration should not be taken light in the sense that it adds value to knowledge value chains, and justifies the effort involved in capture of knowledge in the first place. Hence, knowledge should be centrally available and ideally 'one mouse click away'. Such approach enables 'economies of reuse'. Since web-based access has limitations to transfer of tacit knowledge, it is highly recommended to consider additional mechanisms with complementary value that foster socialization (people-to-people). For this reason, a Project Knowledge Portal (see below) should address linking people based on criteria such as expertise and experience (not to be confused). Keep in mind P2P approaches are prone to project amnesia and are not the dominant strategy in ProwLO.

Project knowledge portal

A Project Knowledge Portal is a tool based on web-based access. It is instrumental in knowledge integration combining the benefits of web-based access with more advanced functions, tailored to specific organizational needs or part of a vendor's product software capability. In the market, Knowledge Portals are generally recognized as company intranets in all their variety. A Project Knowledge Portal could be considered as a special class of such knowledge/information portals focusing on project knowledge and knowledge reuse. Tailor-made, customer business case-driven, knowledge portals (up-to-date) often do not capture the very essence of a Project Knowledge Portal. The obvious explanation is that organizations commissioning such projects lack(ed) access to a thorough conceptual framework, such as ProwLO, promoting the concept of project knowledge and knowledge reuse.

The alternative for a knowledge portal is a stand-alone corporate knowledge base that fully supports ProwLO processes and key concepts, with all their implications. A commercial solution should also pay attention to the different knowledge types possible, not just focus on, say, best practices and lessons learned.

KNOWLEDGE APPLICATION

Case-based reasoning

Foundations of CBR

'Case-based Reasoning' (CBR) is a mechanism to support direction, and thereby knowledge application. According to Watson (2001), CBR is not an AI technology such as logic programming, rule-based reasoning or neural computing, but instead it is a methodology for problem solving. More specifically, Case-based reasoning is a problem-solving paradigm that is able to utilize the specific knowledge of previously experienced, concrete situations (Ribeiro, 2005, p. 3). A key feature of CBR is its coupling to learning. Ribeiro (2005) explains that learning from experience in CBR happens as a natural by-product of problem solving. He also adds that learning is an intrinsic part of CBR because the solutions to past problems and their outcomes are stored as cases to extend the reasoner's knowledge.

The CBR methodology, as suggested by Watson (2001), is a cycle consisting of six activities (the six-REs): 1. Retrieve, 2. Reuse, 3. Revise, 4. Review, 5. Retain and 6. Refine. See Figure 13 for a graphical depiction of Watson's cycle. The agent (i.e. reasoner) retrieves a case to solve a particular problem and attempts to reuse it. This may lead to revision or adaptation of the case's solution resulting in new episodic data and hence a new case being created. The new case is reviewed (involving comparing it against cases already retained in the case-base), and if it is judged useful, it is retained. In addition, the use of the case (successfully or otherwise) may trigger refinement (Watson, 2001). So knowledge evaluation is part of the methodology.

CBR as part of the KM system

CBR can be applied to multiple domains, including project management. Sun et al. (2003) were first to address CBR in the context of management support. They found that traditional approaches were unable to represent managerial events, but were convinced that CBR systems

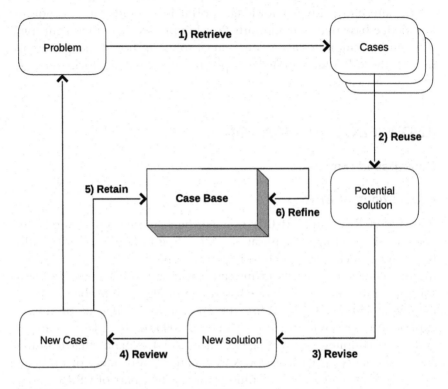

Figure 13 The CBR-Cycle (Watson, 2001, p. 3).

are useful in solving ill-structured problems common in management. So they developed a new model based on 'scenarios' (scenario-based knowledge representation) that covers 'path dependency' and 'context sensitivity'. Path dependency corresponds to the repeated process of 'decision–implementation–feedback–decision', which constitutes the basic content of managerial events. Context sensitivity is a characteristic of managerial events that (always) causes predefined premises to fail in the domain of managerial decision-making since management expertise may not be generalized beyond contexts (Sun et al., 2003, p. 93).

Both aspects of path dependency and context sensitivity can be found in the Cases-method for project management, which can be used to fill the Case base. Corresponding to path dependency, the Cases-method captures scenarios based on decisions and project behaviour and supports iteration, while context sensitivity is manifested in the identification of situational and emergent factors that add to the uniqueness of a situation, but also the retaining of the project context through meta-data, enabling the conception of project similarity useful to the reasoner. The key difference between CBR enabled by the Cases-method as part of ProwLO and Sun et al.'s approach relates to knowledge acquisition and the creation of new Cases. In Sun et al.'s approach, relevant information is extracted from narrative text and reconstructed as basic scenario and linkage units, which can be used to represent Case scenarios, whereas is in ProwLO, Cases are acquired directly as the result of applying the Cases-method. The outcome of the method is a data model of a particular Case.

Case-based Reasoning as a process is enabled by web-based access, i.e. web-based retrieval of Cases. Hence, a web-based implementation of CBR is proposed (Ribeiro, 2005). A Project Knowledge Portal is a perfect tool for searching Cases based on various criteria (e.g. knowledge areas). When the user finds a useful Case, he or she may adopt or adapt solutions (in our case management interventions) that have been successfully applied in the past. However, managers should also learn from negative experience. Therefore, the reasoning process may involve success stories as well as failures. Eventually, the process may result in a new Case. *Evaluating* the Case Base may raise awareness of the need to capture specific experience gained in a particular project. In this sense, CBR is also a potential trigger for knowledge capture, which should not be underestimated.

CBR has a clear benefit for project management as project managers do not have to rely entirely on their own experiences in problem solving, or on the sharing of experiences with others in personal networks. If a particular Case is not directly useful, it may at least direct to someone who has experienced something similar (the key actor of a particular case). Hence, CBR may indirectly foster socialization. But there are also potential pitfalls. Depending on context-sensitivity of project management, Cases may provide limited direction. And the effectiveness of CBR depends on the quality of the captured Cases.

Project approach

The Project Approach is a formal PRINCE2 product and contains a definition of the type of solution to be developed *and* method(ology) of delivering that solution, depending on the former. Experience may provide the rationale for selecting a particular approach. Hence, a Project Approach may rely on Best practices and Lessons Learned. In terms of a KM mechanism, it is a routine that supports knowledge application by promoting knowledge reuse. A key aspect in defining the Project Approach is to map the different options, weigh their advantages and disadvantages and then select the best options.

Although it is desirable to elaborate a formal approach as much as possible, not every detail has to be documented. The key thing is to consider best practices and experiences and to use that knowledge in the project; in other words, to embed the knowledge in the project itself. In this sense, the Project Approach may trigger consideration of existing organizational knowledge in general. The Project Approach partly depends on – but may stimulate as well – the capture of previous lessons, a PRINCE2 activity, prior to selection of elements and definition of a cohesive approach, which is ought to remain stable during the execution of the project (unlike for example the dynamic Project Plan) for consistent processes. In some projects, the end product, however, may be subject to great changes – especially, when the requirements are not clear from the outset. Under such conditions, the Project Approach should incorporate flexibility from the outset, not necessarily a dynamic approach reacting to change, but one that deals with project change most effectively in a stable project management environment.

The Project Approach may, for example, address tailoring and scaling the organizational methodology for managing projects. Tailoring involves modification of process elements at a fundamental level, addressing unsuitability of certain parts of the generic method embedded organizationally, to the point of inadequacy – potentially triggering evolution of this reusable knowledge type of grand scope, and related supporting knowledge objects. This once again calls for an interface based on project feedback. The type of modification triggered by tailoring may involve adopting process elements from different methodologies/methods, developed in-house or available publicly (and there are plenty of alternatives, depending on the industry). It should be noted that some methods are hybrid models that incorporate both management and more technically oriented delivery practices aligned with the solution to be delivered (this can be seen, for example, in IT). Tailoring methods are not trivial and may call for project support, capable of formal definition of process (e.g. using techniques like process-data diagrams), possibly inspired by situational method engineering. Tailoring a generic method has great impact and requires adjustment of project members, another challenge that also involves knowledge integration. Scaling, on the other hand, is a more light-weight approach which involves tuning formality (with implications for communication and work flow) and minor adjustments to process elements (e.g. combining activities or responsibilities), which are allowed within the parameters of the overall method, based on project attributes such as size, complexity, risk, importance and capability. Sometimes, a methodology provides guidance in scaling or even tailoring to some degree, like PRINCE2. PRINCE2 even acknowledges limitations to its generic qualities.

Critical for ProwLO is to be included in the Project Approach. Adopting PRINCE2 as the main project management method is also favourable in the context of ProwLO. To satisfy the requirements of ProwLO, at the very least, a hybrid model with elements of PRINCE2 is essential. Without a formal project management approach, it is difficult to standardize project knowledge management.

Generally, it can be assumed that the Project Approach enables systematic integration of organizational knowledge in project processes. From the perspective of knowledge evaluation, it may also lead to the discovery of knowledge gaps, triggering knowledge development activities.

Standards

Standards are a typical example of routine supporting knowledge application (Becerra et al., 2004). They foster knowledge reuse of a variety of knowledge types, from complete methodologies to single items such as particular Templates, sometimes based on the former. In particular, the broader frameworks (like methods, methodologies, and bodies of knowledge) are either promoted by formal institutions (e.g. ISO) or marketed by commercially oriented associations and organizations seeking public status for their 'product', namely de facto acknowledgement of it being a Standard, industry wide or even across industries. For example, Axelos has made a claim for PRINCE2 being a generic method for any type of project. But in practice, it has to compete with sometimes conflicting industry-specific alternatives, such as Agile approaches in the IT industry. Anticipating the agile trend, Axelos launched PRINCE2-Agile in 2015 to meet new demands of flexibility and responsiveness. Axelos secondly anticipatedby placing more emphasis on tailoring of the core method. PRINCE2: 2009 had a whole chapter devoted to this topic, and the 2017 edition pays even more attention to it. Finally, organizations may develop and use their own custom-made Standards, e.g. based on best practices as they internally evolved.

Standard templates have both advantages and disadvantages. One advantage is that standard templates contribute to a degree of commonality across projects, which organizations generally prefer. Another one is that they help to design and subsequently implement in projects a standardized project management environment aligned with the organizationally embedded methodology, which is especially useful to inexperienced project managers. In other words, the introduction of templates can support education of project practitioners. The biggest limitation, however, is that standard templates cannot precisely match individual projects; the level of detail in documentation is either too little or too great for each project. The solution to this problem is to tailor templates according to project needs, but this may require formal approval (e.g. given in the context of the Project Approach and by Project Board authorization or by the Quality Assurance function, as a generic policy or ad hoc consent). Another disadvantage of templates is that they may lead to unregulated standard *text*, i.e. the verbatim copying of text on subsequent projects, along with the risk that the text is inappropriate or incorrect in subsequent projects.

Generally, standards foster knowledge reuse, i.e. exploitation of knowledge. Mitigating dependency on key individuals, as overall proficiency, will be raised. But also they prevent reinventing the wheel, in terms of practice rooted in process-based methodologies. The main drawback is that strictly following standards may result in suboptimal solutions considering the uniqueness of projects.

REFINE KNOWLEDGE NEEDS

Initiating a Project, recall the parallel process to Establish a Knowledge Processing Framework and first official project Stage, triggers new knowledge and information needs. Not only for IP itself but also for the continuing Stages. The reason for addressing other Stages is that the Project Plan, first created in IP, should take into account related knowledge activities, essential to achieve primary project goals (based on knowledge requirements *in* the project). But if possible, also activities with organizational scope in the context of organizational learning. So, the Project Knowledge Manager should address new knowledge needs as they emerge during IP, particularly focusing on needs that require additional knowledge activities based on discovery of knowledge or experience gaps (at project or organizational level). At the same time, having a better picture of overall knowledge needs will help avoid planning knowledge activities that are in fact manifestations of reinventing the wheel. This applies to knowledge development and capture. Only by mapping out new knowledge needs a planned knowledge gap analysis can be performed, which may provide the rational for developing and capturing knowledge. Knowledge acquisition, from internal and external sources, also solves knowledge gaps. If knowledge – along with expertise – needs to be acquired from external sources, the Project Plan should take this into account, in a similar fashion to procurement of external products, with all its implications for project processes. The Project Knowledge Manager should also refine the knowledge needs captured so far (based on SU).

Foresight of knowledge needs enables better integration of KM activities in project planning and their effective execution in Stages. A sub-activity of refining knowledge needs is to update live tracking, adding knowledge needs as entities in a support tool for monitoring and control purposes.

UPDATE KM ACTIVITIES PLAN

Based on the refined list of knowledge needs, the KM activity plan needs to be updated. For each new knowledge need, all knowledge processes, as part of the PKVC, should be taken into consideration.

Recommended IP knowledge activities include:

- Refer to example Project Initiation Documents, specifically examining:
  - Strategies for Risk Management, Quality Management, Configuration Management, Communication, as addressed in PRINCE2, and Knowledge Management inspired by ProwLO.
  - Project controls.
  - The base-lined Project Plan (as opposed to the related dynamic entity).
  - The base-lined Business Case (as opposed to the related dynamic entity).
  - The adopted KM system.
- Refer to example Project Plans with factual data for more realistic planning (final versions at the end of projects).
- Refer to example mature Business Cases (which are more reliable).
- Apply estimation techniques using historical data, if industry applicable and supported by organizational processes.
- Apply other Project Planning techniques.

- Validate the adopted KM system – in terms of feasibility – against past definitions found in sample PIDs and sufficient organizational support currently to effectively carry out ProwLO activities. If ProwLO is formally adopted as part of the strategy and generally accepted in the organization but insufficiently supported, raise an issue for organizational change beyond project boundaries with or without endorsement of the Project Board who has to deal with the proposed KM system.
- Tailor the PID template integrated in SU according to project needs.

EVALUATE KNOWLEDGE NEEDS SATISFACTION INITIATING A PROJECT

Evaluating knowledge needs satisfaction IP is essentially identical to evaluation in SU; only now it concerns different knowledge needs. Recall that it is a knowledge process that may trigger to define and plan new activities, now in the context of Updating the KM activity Plan, causing a new iteration. In the following Stages involving technical phases, this activity is no longer an explicit part of the ProwLO process model. Evaluating knowledge needs satisfaction is namely superceded by monitoring knowledge value chains in the context of Live Capture (see Chapter 7, section 'Monitoring Knowledge Value Chains'), parallel to Controlling a Stage, based on greater value proposition taking into account organizational scope as opposed to project-specific Stage knowledge needs.

EXECUTE IP KNOWLEDGE ACTIVITIES

Similar to evaluating knowledge needs, executing knowledge activities in IP does not essentially differ from the corresponding process in SU. In the following Stages involving technical phases, this type of process corresponds to 'Execute Stage Knowledge Activities', in the context of Live Capture. In the following Stages, the execution process is driven by updated KM activity plans, maintained during 'Trigger Knowledge Value chains' parallel to Managing Stage Boundaries and updated at the beginning of Live Capture (as new Stages commence), in which the Stage Plan should take into account specific knowledge activities with Stage impact. In Establishing the Knowledge Processing Framework, in contrast, the overall Project Impact of the KM activity plan – thus far – should be examined (in combination with the KM strategy and KM system), the next activity of this ProwLO process.

EXAMINE PROJECT PLAN IMPACT

One aspect of Project Planning is to allocate time and resources for the delivery of management products according to the requirements of the project management environment. Similarly, planning should incorporate efforts necessary to perform knowledge activities, aimed at manipulating knowledge needs, their corresponding knowledge value chains and supporting reusable knowledge objects, according to project knowledge management requirements aligned with and supported by the same environment. All of the defined knowledge activities should support or try not to be in conflict with the KM strategy. The KM system that follows strategy should enable or facilitate these activities. Project Planning provides a pragmatic opportunity to validate such activities against the capabilities of the KM system currently in place. A Project Plan namely has to be feasible with realistic estimates and this also applies to knowledge activities. Solving a knowledge gap might be critical but fundamental process support may be lacking. For example, if you never capture a particular type of experience, the knowledge gap may persist at organizational level, increasing dependence on key individuals. If so, planning may address KM initiatives to enhance the KM system, either based on project mandate and executed as a sub-project or an organizational mandate for an external project yet to be instantiated for parallel, interface to the current project, or future execution. ProwLO capability relies on the KM system and its proficiency depends on process knowledge. So, training the project team, in particular the project manager and project knowledge manager, in the ProwLO process model together with key concepts of the KM system could be an important precondition for successful execution of particular knowledge activities, and thus be included in the Project Plan. Based on the overall assessment of project plan impact, the Project Plan can be created or updated in the context of Initiating a Project.

UPDATE PROJECT INITIATION DOCUMENT

The final activity of Establish a Knowledge Management Framework is to update the Project Initiation Document. This involves attachment of the KM strategy and KM system as defined earlier in this process. The Project Board then authorizes the project based on a fundamental understanding of project knowledge management as part of the project management environment and Project Approach in particular.

IMPLICATIONS FOR OTHER FRAMEWORKS

Table 10 relates Establish Knowledge Processing with the Praxis Framework, PMBok and the ARCADIS process model.

Table 10 Establish Knowledge Processing Implications for Other Frameworks

PRINCE2 activity with ProwLO interface	Framework	Corresponding process element of alternative framework
Create Project Plan	Praxis	Plan Delivery. Praxis states that the content and extent of this activity are unique to each project and programme. According to this method, there are various planning documents addressing aspects of planning (e.g. scheduling, risk, stakeholders, resources and financials). So, unlike in PRINCE2, the project plan is not necessarily a single entity.
	PMBoK	Develop Project Management Plan as part of the Planning Process Group and mapped with Project Integration Management.
	ARCADIS	As main contractor, ARCADIS has to manage both the customer project and the internal project, driven by the Business Case for ARCADIS only. Accordingly, ARCADIS makes use of an internal Project Plan, created in the context of 'Project Leadership and Project Management', a high-level process. The customer Project Plan, on the other hand,

(Continued)

Table 10 (Cont.)

PRINCE2 activity with ProwLO interface	Framework	Corresponding process element of alternative framework
		is part of delivery work and often involves specialist Planners, due to the complexity of engineering projects. Sometimes, it is part of a framework agreement. The internal Project Plan relies on a process called Capacity Planning, which corresponds to the management of resources.

Table 11 relates roles to activities in Establish Knowledge Processing.

Table 11 Establish Knowledge Processing Suggested Roles and Responsibilities

Activity/Role	Project Knowledge Manager	Project Manager	Project Board	1. Project Team Members 2. Chief Knowledge Officer 3. PMO
Prepare KM Strategy	Producer Attaches to Project Initiation Document (PID)	Reviewer Updates PID, adding attachment	Reader Reviewer in the context of project authorization based on Project Initiation Document*	2. Defines corporate KM strategy, used as input in this activity
Setup Knowledge Management System	Document combination of KM mechanisms and technologies to support the project	Reviewer Updates PID, adding attachment	Reader	2. Identifies the need for new KM initiatives aligned with the project's defined KM strategy and system

(*Continued*)

Table 11 (Cont.)

Activity/Role	Project Knowledge Manager	Project Manager	Project Board	1. Project Team Members 2. Chief Knowledge Officer 3. PMO
	Implement the system for ready use			supporting the chosen strategy 3. Prepares infrastructure, including IT tools, to realize setup of the proposed KM system
Refine Knowledge Needs	Updating documented knowledge needs (documentation and/or online data)	Review	Reader	–
Update KM Activities Plan	Producer	Reviewer	–	1. Notification and acknowledgement
Evaluate Knowledge Needs Satisfaction	Evaluate. Report to Project Board	Provide input to Project Knowledge Manager	Notified of evaluation results	3. Reviewer and responsible for co-development of key knowledge artefacts
Execute IP Knowledge Activities	Potential involvement	Directing activities based on individual needs	–	3. Co-development of knowledge artefacts, particularly related to project management
Examine Project Plan Impact	Evaluate, a co-responsibility Reviewer	Evaluate, a co-responsibility Producer	Reviewer	1. Engagement of specialist Planners

(*Continued*)

Table 11 (Cont.)

Activity/Role	Project Knowledge Manager	Project Manager	Project Board	1. Project Team Members 2. Chief Knowledge Officer 3. PMO
Update Project Initiation Document			Reviewer in the context of project authorization based on latest version of the PID	3. Publication of the PID as sample document as to satisfy knowledge needs (an example of knowledge integration), depending on confidentiality of documentation

* Reader stands for 'casual accumulation of information'. As reader, the Project Board is not triggered to react, providing feedback, but driven by knowledge support may do so in an ad hoc fashion.

6 Trigger knowledge value chains

The process of 'Trigger Knowledge Value Chains' runs in parallel with Managing Stage Boundaries (see Figure 14). The concept of knowledge value chains is unprecedented. It could be considered as an object that can be valued and evaluated. This is in line with the fundamental proposition that knowledge has a life cycle and may expire in an ever-changing climate and environment.

Prior to the notion of knowledge value chains, there were some attempts to directly link knowledge management to business performance indicators. A rather false notion. From a statistical point of view, it is very difficult to isolate KM interventions as variables, and thereby, establish proper causal relations (cause and effect). Consequently, business performance indicators are a poor indicator for knowledge management. Besides, there is a clear distinction between KM interventions and KM processing; interdependent but unique in their own kind based on management level (strategic & tactical versus operational). Knowledge value chains reflect operational-level knowledge processing, which can be measured objectively, whilst they address the strategic value of knowledge, based on metrics and in word. There is not a more practical and objective way to measure the value of knowledge management. The impact of KM interventions should simply be derived from the changes in knowledge processing.

REVIEW KNOWLEDGE NEEDS' NEXT STAGE

The first activity of Trigger Knowledge Value chains is to review the knowledge needs' next stage. It is triggered either by 'Authorize KM Strategy' in the context of 'Authorize a Project' or 'Review Stage

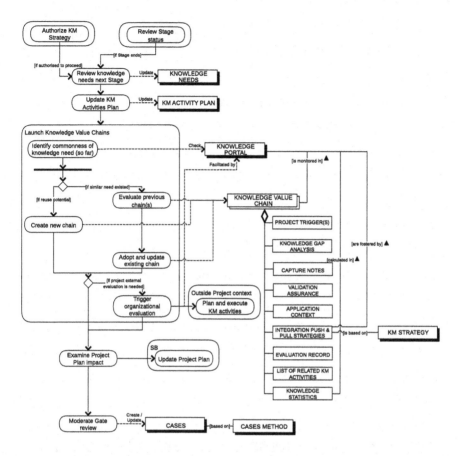

Figure 14 Trigger Knowledge Value Chains.

Status' stemming from Managing Stage Boundaries (SB), provided that the latter activity triggers a transition, namely an approaching end to a stage. Note that PRINCE2 'Review Stage Status' is both event- and time-driven activity (triggered by other activities and time elapse). And not every stage review is followed by Managing a Stage Boundary. For example, in Controlling a Stage, stage reviews also follow 'Review Work Package status'. Just like SB, Trigger Knowledge Value chains is a fixed process with no recursion, repeated only for every new stage as planned or following an Exception Plan (ending the current Stage), as requested by the Project Board. The output of the review on knowledge needs is to update the knowledge needs entities. Different sources can be used as input, including the Stage Plan (or Exception Plan) for the next stage. The Project Knowledge

Manager should take full advantage of the Stage-gate paradigm, opening time for reflection, and take a proactive stance in the process of capturing new knowledge needs.

UPDATE KM ACTIVITIES PLAN

The second activity is to update the KM activity plan, simply based on the newly identified knowledge needs. Special attention should be paid to knowledge gaps analysis. The central questions are: do we know what we do not know, and what is required? And: do we know what we know? What project team members do not know – yet knowing what they need – might be known somewhere else in the organization. The organizational level of such analysis is key in order to prevent reinventing the wheel. The practical implication is that in order to plan KM activities in detail, it might be necessary to answer the two questions first based on requirements and knowledge gap analysis. So the latter knowledge process may be performed in the process of updating the KM activities plan. Once the knowledge needs are established, the team, under the lead of the Project Knowledge Manager, can then start enquiries as to identify whether particular knowledge is present in the organization. The outcome of these enquires may provide justification for planning knowledge development or knowledge capture.

IDENTIFY COMMONNESS OF KNOWLEDGE (SO FAR)

After the above initial process activities, a greater process starts, called 'Launch Knowledge Value Chains'. This process consists of sub-processes, i.e. activities. It is a recursive process in the sense that it is repeated for every single knowledge need not yet associated with a knowledge value chain (the Project Knowledge Manager needs to keep up with this). The first activity is to identify the commonness of knowledge needs, at present and in the future, based on foresight of portfolio changes. "So far" is added because in a dynamic and changing environment with different project owners, knowledge needs change as well. To determine how common a need is, the corporate knowledgebase/knowledge portal should be checked, either by search based on keywords or by browsing. It is unrealistic to assume that all knowledge assets are recorded in a centralized knowledgebase. So, additionally, the Project Knowledge Manager, responsible for the whole process, should do some research by asking fellow colleagues, or ask team members to do the same. It should be noted that centralization of knowledge should not make an organization more vulnerable. Therefore, as a safeguard to knowledge leaks, data loss, and other forms of data corruption, attention should be payed to data security. Despite the risks, one can imagine that centralization leads to greater effectiveness and efficiency based on simple economies of scale (with information as resource). Arguably, a centralized system supported by a centralized infrastructure enables having the right knowledge at the right time and in the right place, simply based on easy and quick access of data whenever required. What should be added to this one-liner, however, is 'right person', giving greater meaning to data accessibility and data security.

After this activity what automatically follows is a decision tree, either a similar need already existed (monitored or not, present in an IT system or not) or a new need has been discovered *with* reuse potential. In case of the former, the activity that follows is to evaluate previous chains, facilitated by a knowledge portal (or corporate knowledge base supporting knowledge value chain entities). In case of the latter, a new Knowledge Value Chain is created from scratch based on the key knowledge need.

CREATE NEW CHAIN

The activity of 'Create a new chain' is straightforward based on understanding of the concept of Knowledge Value Chain. This complex concept consists of the following attributes (i.e. components):

- Project trigger.
- Knowledge gap analysis (most likely there is a gap, the current need needs to be satisfied by performing KM activities).
- Capture notes (ranging from logbook entry to the wider context of the knowledge need from any angle as creative as it may get).
- Validation assurance (if there is an answer to the knowledge need, it has to be validated properly by the right authorities and experts).
- Application context. Knowledge has a use; it is not simple information like news that is not actual and or actionable.
- Integration of Push and Pull Strategies. This attribute links the knowledge value with the ProwLO product of KM strategy, established in Establishing Knowledge Processing. Pull and Push are, in other words, integration strategies that should be in line with the chosen KM strategy, favourably fully supporting ProwLO.

- Evaluation record. The application or use of a knowledge value chain, strongly depending on the associated (reusable) information knowledge object, may vary over time. This will be without doubt reflected by an evaluation record, if taken care of.
- List of related KM activities. All actions of the associated reusable knowledge object are recorded here. The majority of KM activities are probably already defined in the KM Activities Plan, earlier in the process, so use this plan as input.
- Knowledge statistics. Knowledge value chain statistics are not the same as reusable knowledge need (object) statistics, first identified in Initiate Knowledge Processes. There is, however, an overlap based on the fact that knowledge objects are associated with value chains. In either case, monitoring based on the number of clicks works the same.

EVALUATE PREVIOUS CHAIN(S)

In case a similar need has been identified earlier and complemented with a value chain entity, this similar chain needs to be evaluated. It is possible that there is more than one similar chain. This could be caused by, for example, duplication and ambiguous entries (making picking more difficult). In such a case, the most suitable one should be chosen for adoption based on user-defined criteria. Examples of criteria are more suitable knowledge objects associated with a particular chain (given specific project needs), or longer monitoring period with greater knowledge statistics.

ADOPT AND UPDATE CHAIN

Following evaluation of existing chains, the most suitable chain has to be adopted. This adoption entails adding a new project trigger (e.g. by means of a project identification number) and updating attributes. Hence, a knowledge value chain is a dynamic entity, yet one that persists over time. In contrast, knowledge needs are also dynamic but may stop being actual at a particular moment in time, stopping the need for reusable knowledge objects as well. If that happens, no one may notice. Knowledge value chains, on the other hand, claim that specific knowledge had use (and thus, value) in the past, could be useful in the present and also may have potential use in the future depending on dynamic portfolio needs, as it had reuse potential in the first place.

TRIGGER ORGANIZATIONAL EVALUATION

The decision tree as part of launch knowledge value chain is two-fold. It involves two decisions which are straightforward given a particular context and assessment of the situation. The first one is explained above: adopting an existing knowledge value chain or creating a new one. The second decision is near the end of launching knowledge value chains as the choice is presented to 'Trigger Organizational Evaluation'. The latter activity is performed only if project external evaluation is required, for example, for knowledge validation purposes. What happens then is that KM activities are planned outside the scope of the project, not taking any project time, with clever resource management. These activities are not necessarily post-project activities; they could be performed concurrent to the managed project, e.g. in the context of Communities of Practice.

EXAMINE PROJECT PLAN IMPACT

After 'Launch Knowledge Value Chain', the next activity is 'Evaluate Project Plan Impact', taking into consideration knowledge value chains and associated KM activities planned for the next Stage. In PRINCE2, it is natural that the Project Plan is dynamic based on the creation of new Stage Plan and Exception Plan. So, modification of the Project Plan due to triggering knowledge value chains nicely fits with Managing Stage Boundaries. In other words, there is an interface with PRINCE2 and the Project Plan gets to be updated prior to the next stage.

MODERATE GATE REVIEW

The final process activity is to moderate Gate Reviews which may lead to the capture of Cases (see Chapter 5, section 'Knowledge Capture', sub-section 'Cases-method'). The Stage-Gate model favoured by and required for ProwLO allows this to happen. This activity is perfect as an organizational routine for knowledge capture. It complements the *live* capture of Cases in the process (also) called Live Capture, presented in the next chapter. As discussed in Chapter 5, applying the Cases-method at key decision moments has the benefit that feedback processes can be better analysed, based on hindsight, as there is more time to reflect. Compared to Postcontrol, when a project is closing, Gate Reviews do not suffer from project amnesia in the same measure. Especially, long and complex projects suffer from memory loss and fragmentation. Root causes include changing team membership during the course of a project, or worse, personnel turnover.

IMPLICATIONS FOR OTHER FRAMEWORKS

The second big limitation of PMBoK, aside from the lack of a sponsorship process, is the lack of a distinct and elaborated boundaries process, such as found in PRINCE2 or Praxis Framework. The activity of 'Close Project or *Phase*' is the only reference to a similar concept in this body of knowledge. While PRINCE2 takes full advantage of the stage-gate paradigm, Praxis approach is more conservative based on the observation that delivery often shows overlap making it difficult to draw boundaries. While it is true that technical phases may overlap one another or be executed in parallel, the definition of stages should primarily be based on key decision moments, in line with the PRINCE2 principle of manage-by-stages. Hence, devolution of the stage-gate paradigm as seen in Praxis is not recommended. In the context of ProwLO, a boundaries process is fundamental.

Table 12 relates Trigger Knowledge Value Chains with the Praxis Framework, PMBok and the ARCADIS process model.

Table 12 Trigger Knowledge Value Chains Implications for Other Frameworks

PRINCE2 activity with ProwLO interface	*Framework*	*Corresponding process element of alternative framework*
Review Stage Status as trigger of Review knowledge needs' next stage, in the context of managing a stage boundary (when a stage is closing to an end)	Praxis	No explicit reference to this activity. Most related is the delivery process of 'Coordinate and monitor progress'. It is essential that the latter has an interface with the Praxis Boundaries process (not just the delivery process as a whole), triggering Review knowledge needs' next stage as part of a stage transition. That the boundaries process is a sub-process of delivery – not a distinct process like in PRINCE2 at the same level as Controlling a Stage – is of less importance. One of the reasons, probably, why the boundaries process is engrained in the

(Continued)

Table 12 (Cont.)

PRINCE2 activity with ProwLO interface	Framework	Corresponding process element of alternative framework
		delivery process is that Praxis argues that tranches of work often overlap, across stages. ProwLO, on the other hand, acknowledges key decision moments as what separates stages from one another, while technical phases may take a different course (such as show overlap across stages – one phase starts before the previous ends – or parallel execution). The distinction between stages and technical phases is adopted from PRINCE2
	PMBoK	There is no corresponding activity in PMBoK. The closest defined activity is 'Monitor and control project work', which is multi-faceted. The issue is that it is not followed by a boundaries process. Hence, PMBoK is unable to trigger Review knowledge needs' next Stage
	ARCADIS	ARCADIS defines a high-level process of Monitoring and Control. Just like PMBoK, it does not define a boundaries process
Update Project Plan	Praxis	There is no distinct Update Project Plan activity. Instead, the activity of 'Plan next tranche/stage' should take into account knowledge value chains and planned KM activities
	PMBoK	Although PMBoK addresses Closing a phase, the guidance is very minimalistic and not a true boundaries process. Instead of updating a Project Plan, PMBoK states that the activity of Close Project or Phase uses a project management plan as one of its inputs. So here it is by no means dynamic, as a project moves from one stage to another
	ARCADIS	As mentioned above, ARCADIS has no boundaries process. Updating the Project Plan before the start of a new stage is therefore not a standard procedure

SUGGESTED ROLES AND RESPONSIBILITIES

Table 13 relates roles to activities in Trigger Knowledge Value Chains.

Table 13 Trigger Knowledge Value Chains Suggested Roles and Responsibilities

Activity/Role	Project Knowledge Manager	Project Manager	Project Board	1. Project Team Members 2. Chief Knowledge Officer 3. PMO
Review Knowledge Needs' next Stage	Update identified knowledge needs	Review	Reader	1. Enquiry of individual team members 3. PMO as project support: Review of updated knowledge needs, particularly focusing on management knowledge
Update KM Activities Plan	Updates	Reviewer	Reader	1. Involved individuals' acknowledgement
Identify Commonness of Knowledge Need (so far)	Check knowledge portal. Start enquiries. Draw conclusion based on available data	Reviewer	Reader	1. Provide confirmation if necessary
Create New Chain	Producer	Reviewer	Reader	1. Subject matter experts validate the knowledge value chain entities

(*Continued*)

Table 13 (Cont.)

Activity/Role	Project Knowledge Manager	Project Manager	Project Board	1. Project Team Members 2. Chief Knowledge Officer 3. PMO
Evaluate Previous Chain(s)	Evaluate	–	–	–
Adopt and Update Existing Chain	Update	Approve	Reader	–
Trigger Organizational Evaluation	Trigger	Endorse	Notified	1. Subject matter experts in Communities of Practice are contacted for planning KM activities outside the project context
Examine Project Plan Impact	Evaluate Share findings with Project Manager	Updates Project Plan	Focuses on Managing a Stage Boundary	–
Moderate Gate Reviews	Facilitates Gate Reviews Produces Cases based on Cases-method	Involved in capture of project management Cases	Reviews captured Cases	1. May participate in meetings and ask questions for data collection Possibly engage in validity checks as subject matter experts

7 Live capture

Live Capture, parallel to Controlling a Stage, is primarily a knowledge capture process associated with knowledge value chains. It mainly serves providing triggers for actual knowledge development, especially the capture of newly gained experience. During the course of a Stage, knowledge capture is a continuous process. This also applies to three parallel ProwLO sub-processes as part of Live Capture, namely 1) directing knowledge capture, 2) monitoring knowledge value chains (in which captured information is directly linked to existing knowledge value chains records) and 3) execution of stage knowledge activities (complementing formal capture). In addition, three activities are performed once at the beginning of every Stage. Namely, 'Identify Organizational Knowledge Needs', 'Identify Project and Individual Knowledge Gaps' and 'Identify repeated nature of Stage Issues'. The activity of 'Evaluate Knowledge Application' is performed near the end of the Stage, but also can be triggered by 'Evaluate Specialist Knowledge Reuse' during the Stage. Finally, if planned, 'Report Knowledge Needs Satisfaction' is the final sub-process, performed at the very end of Live Capture, also near the end of the Stage. See Figure 15 for a graphical representation.

The three initial activities provide a wider context for knowledge capture in an organization. First of all, knowledge capture is based on organizational knowledge needs (not necessarily the project's), of which the majority are undocumented (unless documented or recorded in knowledge value chains). Second, project knowledge experience gaps are identified. The focus here is the project itself instead of the organization as a whole. This involves experience gaps at personal level,

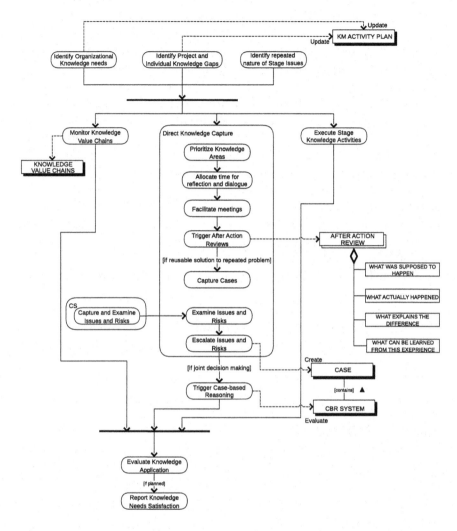

Figure 15 Live Capture.

spotting the weakest links (not for personal scapegoating but to assist and for growth). Third and finally, Issues that tend to repeat or remain unresolved are identified. These Issues are potential Cases, a knowledge type that greatly assists decision-making. By carrying out these prior activities, the process of knowledge capture becomes much more predictable and directing easier. In the process, the KM activity plan is updated. More details on the specific sub-processes are provided in the subsequent sections.

IDENTIFY ORGANIZATIONAL KNOWLEDGE NEEDS

In order to assess organizational knowledge needs properly, you need to know what you know (e.g. by documenting available knowledge) and, second, what you do *not* know (based on what is required), a simple knowledge gap analysis at the organizational level. If you do not know what you know at the organizational level (the bigger an organization, the more complex to assess), there is a high probability you will end up reinventing the wheel. It is by no means an excess to understand as much as possible in the business, from environment to supply chain in operation. Based on portfolio awareness, the assessment should be directed at inter-project learning. And based on portfolio developments, the assessment should also take into account future knowledge needs. This requires an interface with the enterprise function of Portfolio Management, and more specifically, an information flow from. Interesting portfolio data include project types and volume of projects.

In the process of identifying organizational knowledge needs, the KM activity plan is updated. Newly planned activities defined in this plan will affect the current Stage. Modification of Team Plans may be applicable.

IDENTIFY PROJECT AND INDIVIDUAL KNOWLEDGE GAPS

Unlike the process of Project Establishment (i.e. formation of the project management team and allocation of specialists), identification of knowledge gaps at the project and individual levels is an ad hoc ongoing process. The two are compared because in the process of team formation, knowledge and experience gaps are intentionally avoided by selecting the right people. Once a team is formed and becomes stable, limitations of individuals become fixed, unless a new member joins the team to address particular weaknesses, and learning is not a viable option. Assigning new team members is just one way to cope with the dynamic nature of projects, that is to say change. Every project deals with change and emergent factors. The other way to cope with change is team ability to adjust to emergent knowledge gaps. As identified knowledge gaps enable focused learning knowledge gaps can be resolved.

IDENTIFY REPEATED NATURE OF STAGE ISSUES

Identification of Stage Issues that tend to repeat is unlike 'Examine Issues and Risks' which may trigger 'Direct Knowledge Capture' (see below), a one-time event (per stage). The difference is that the former activity takes into account all previous Stages as well as Issues based on historical data and concurrent projects as part of a portfolio, whereas the latter focus on the use of an Issue Log and takes into account only the current Stage. The outcome of this activity is increased management control – a capability, not a document or record. Essentially, two types of issues can be identified: issues that are common across projects (i.e. organizational level), and issues that repeat – or remain unsolved – as the project moves from one stage to another. Common issues are generally a basic knowledge need, a knowledge type so to say.

DIRECT KNOWLEDGE CAPTURE

Directing knowledge capture is a key responsibility of the Project Knowledge Manager. It starts with the sub-process of: 'Prioritize knowledge areas'. Every reusable knowledge need belongs to a domain and is further categorized by a sub-domain, i.e. area. Next, time should be allocated for dialogue and discussion. Socialization may help better understanding and finding common interests. As capture takes significant time, it has to be fully supported. Socialization is formally embedded as 'Facilitate meetings', the next activity. In case of urgent Stage Cases, the Project Knowledge Manager role may trigger 'After Action Reviews' (AAR), a technique used in the military after things went wrong. Recall that an AAR consists of four pieces of information:

- What was supposed to happen.
- What actually happened.
- An explanation of the difference (address both situational and emergent factors).
- What can be learned from this experience.

Hence, AAR automatically results in Lessons Learned to be recorded in the Lessons Log, and later in the Lessons Learned Report.

If a similar problem repeats across projects and if there is a reusable potential solution, the Project Knowledge Manager takes care of the development of a Case, preferably captured based on a Template or recorded on tape/video.

Directing Knowledge Capture is not only a flow of events anticipating knowledge needs and issues, but also event-driven by PRINCE2. The PRINCE2 activity of 'Capture and Examine Issues and Risks' triggers a parallel activity for the Project Knowledge Manager in the context of ProwLO. The advantage of this approach is that the PKM can complement the PM's work and discover more Cases (of course, with reuse potential). The PKM has the authority to escalate issues and risk, not as much as to readdress the Project Plan, but to elaborate new Cases derived from these issues and risks. Depending on the domain of the problem – either fundamentally management or specialist – the Project Knowledge Manager should use interviewing techniques – either during meetings or on special occasion – to gather all necessary data in order to produce a Case in all its content. Obviously, for project management Cases, the key interviewee is the Project Manager, who should also be concerned with validation of the captured knowledge (as subject matter expert).

Cases are factual; they occur in practice with or without recording. Generally, project managers or other key decision-makers make decisions and take actions and their outcome can be observed as project behaviour. The capture of Cases can aid actual decision-making as Cases are a tool for problem solving. Based on rational analysis, the captured data may help to identify better alternatives. The creation of new Cases in the context of 'Escalate Issues and Risks' is the final process activity belonging to 'Direct Knowledge Capture'.

TRIGGER CASE-BASED REASONING

Sometimes, Cases are so complex that they need additional deliberation, provided they were addressed in the first place during general meetings or short interviews. In such cases, Case-Based Reasoning should be applied (see Chapter 5, section 'Knowledge Application', sub-section 'Case-based Reasoning'), in a social setting like joint decision-making, the next process activity. A tool for effective and efficient retrieval and evaluation of Cases is paramount here.

MONITOR KNOWLEDGE VALUE CHAINS

Parallel to directing knowledge capture is monitoring knowledge value chains. Every project should contain a dashboard (supported by a tool) with all relevant knowledge value chains. As Live Capture draws on all generic knowledge processes that are part of the knowledge value chain (primarily driven by Stage activity), a lot of information can be of added value to individual knowledge chain entities.

EXECUTE STAGE ACTIVITIES AND EVALUATE KNOWLEDGE APPLICATION

Also parallel to directing knowledge capture is the execution of Stage Activities, planned earlier. When all three parallel processes come together near Stage End, there is an opportunity to evaluate knowledge application, including the reuse of knowledge or lack of it. The outside trigger of this activity is 'Evaluate Specialist Knowledge Reuse', from the ProwLO process Reuse specialist knowledge. Ideally, this trigger is near the end of the Stage for better synchronization and clearer hindsight.

REPORT KNOWLEDGE NEED SATISFACTION

At the very end, the Project Knowledge Manager reports knowledge needs satisfaction to the Project Board. This activity is self-explanatory. A negative report may induce closer observation by the Project Board and greater ad hoc (knowledge based) direction, also a ProwLO activity.

IMPLICATIONS FOR OTHER FRAMEWORKS

Table 14 relates Live Capture with the Praxis Framework, PMBok and the ARCADIS process model.

Table 14 Live Capture Implications for Other Frameworks

PRINCE2 activity with ProwLO interface	Framework	Corresponding process element of alternative framework
Capture and Examine Issues and Risks	Praxis	There is no explicit reference to this activity. It is therefore an implicit responsibility of the Project Manager in the context of 'Co-ordinate and monitor progress'. In any case, The Project Knowledge Manager

(*Continued*)

Table 14 (Cont.)

PRINCE2 activity with ProwLO interface	*Framework*	*Corresponding process element of alternative framework*
		should be aware (e.g. based on analysis and latest updates of the Issue and Risk Log, both PRINCE2 products) or made aware as to complement the Project Manager
	PMBoK	The Issue Log is an output of Manage Stakeholder engagement and is used as input in the activities of Manage Project Team (identified as a human resources challenge), Control communications and Control Stakeholder Engagement. With its specific purpose, it appears to lack a broader scope and application context. Examination of risks, and more generally risk management, on the other hand, is dealt with separately. It is a distinct knowledge area and as such has extensive coverage. So, a distinct activity identical to 'Capture and Examine Issues and Risks', and it should be stressed *issues of any kind*, is unfortunately missing
	ARCADIS	The closest reference is the high-level process of Monitoring and Control. Based on an initiative to update the ARCADIS process model, ARCADIS incorporated PRINCE2 elements like the Issue Log. Prior to this, the use of an Issue Log was an informal practice

SUGGESTED ROLES AND RESPONSIBILITIES

Table 15 relates roles to activities in Live Capture.

Table 15 Live Capture Suggested Roles and Responsibilities

Activity/Role	Project Knowledge Manager	Project Manager	Project Board	1. Project Team Members 2. Chief Knowledge Officer 3. PMO
Identify Organizational Knowledge Needs	Update KM Activities Plan	Reader	–	1. Notified of involvement, providing acknowledgement 2. Review 3. Review
Identify Project and Individual Knowledge Gaps	Update KM Activities Plan. Gaps are explicitly referenced in the plan. Communicate discovery of gaps	Reviewer, in the event of newly identified gaps	Reviewer, in the event of newly identified gaps	2. Review, in the event of newly identified gaps. Input for KM strategy Process at corporate level (see Chapter 5, section 'Prepare KM Strategy', sub-section 'Knowledge Strategy Process') 3. Contemplate implications, liaise with human resource management
Identify Repeated Nature of Stage Issues	Capture	Reviewer. Decide to pass on to Project Board or not	Reviewer in the event Project Manager passes information	3. Collect common Issues across projects
Monitor Knowledge Value Chains	Review Knowledge Value Chains entities during a Stage	–	–	–

(Continued)

Table 15 (Cont.)

Activity/Role	Project Knowledge Manager	Project Manager	Project Board	1. Project Team Members 2. Chief Knowledge Officer 3. PMO
Direct Knowledge Capture	Responsible and accountable for the entire process of knowledge capture during a stage	Released from the burden of knowledge capture but still closely involved as to guarantee quality of captured knowledge	Participate in meetings	3. Exchange of insights with Project Knowledge Manager. Support the Project Knowledge Manager with knowledge capture
Prioritize Knowledge Areas	Contemplate. Document	Review	Review	3. Review
Allocate Time for Reflection and Dialogue	Schedule	Approve	Acknowledge	–
Facilitate Meetings	Prepare and facilitate	Participate in meetings	Potentially join meetings	–
Trigger After Action Reviews	Pitch After Action Review to the team. Trigger this activity. Document report	Show leadership as to prevent blaming culture when things go wrong	Review report	3. Review captured lessons learned
Capture Cases	Produce Cases following After Action Reviews provided that there is a reusable solution to a repeated problem	Review	Reader	3. Validate Case

Examine Issues and Risks	Evaluate	—	—	—
Escalate Issues and Risks	Produce Cases unrelated to executed After Action Reviews	Review	Review. The knowledge type of a Case is also a relevant project management information in this context	3. Validate Case
Trigger Case-based Reasoning	Address added value of CBR to the team. Trigger this process in case of joint decision-making involving multiple actors	Apply	Communicated chosen decision or taken actions	3. Guarantee infrastructure and systems supporting CBR as part of the corporate KM system
Execute Stage Knowledge Activities	Observation	Embed in planning. And address in High-Light Report for the Project Board	Review High-Light Report	—
Evaluate Knowledge Application	Evaluate. Communicate findings with Project Manager	Review. Pass on or not to the board	Notified of results by Project Manager. Additionally, a Proactive approach as to acquire knowledge reuse findings, in line with Directing Knowledge Processes	3. Enquiry of results based on PMO needs
Report Knowledge Needs Satisfaction	Documentation	Review	Reader	—

8 Reuse specialist knowledge

Reuse specialist knowledge runs in parallel with Managing Product Delivery (see Figure 16). In projects, all sorts of specialists are engaged in specialist work. Sometimes, typical project management activities are also performed by specialists, in particular Planners and Risk Managers, but also Project Knowledge Managers as prescribed by ProwLO. Obviously, technicians in projects are specialists. Arguably, the project manager is foremost a people manager and someone who manages the overall process aligned with available standards based on tailoring requirements. Furthermore, according to Hilary Small, the best project managers focus on business outcomes and business value, while the majority focuses on delivery of the end product and getting things done. In other words, the best managers are less pre-occupied with specialist (read technical) affairs or supported by a technical project manager, depending on the project organization. The latter construction, however, is not usual. The role inherent to technical project management is usually covered by project leaders, or in PRINCE2 terms, team managers. The most obvious reason why project management activities are 'outsourced' is their inherent complexity combined with the availability of staff who is better trained in executing related tasks. Another reason is to ease the burden on project managers through project support. In the latter case, project support may evolve to specialist services. The management versus specialist distinction is adopted from PRINCE2. Of course, based on the unique skills associated with project management, a project manager is a specialist in his or her own right, but this is a matter of definition.

The role of the Project Knowledge Manager is to facilitate reuse of all kinds of specialist knowledge, during and across projects. This is

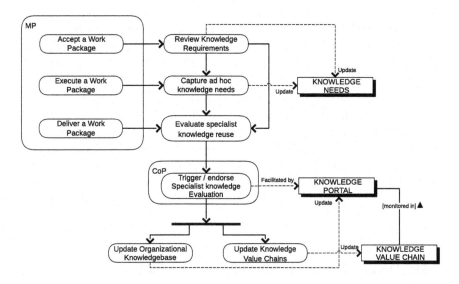

Figure 16 Reuse Specialist Knowledge.

achieved by close cooperation with PRINCE2 Team Managers, or more generally, Project Managers responsible for team management, in the specific context of managing product delivery. It should be noted that Communities of Practice, which are organic and dynamic structures, complement the Project Knowledge Manager in increasing knowledge reuse. The Project Knowledge Manager should be aware of such communities, at intra-organizational level and beyond, because he or she might need their help for interpretation of contextual information. Cooperation with CoP also enables the Project Knowledge Manager to trigger evaluation of specialist knowledge beyond the level of single projects, as may follow from the Reuse specialist knowledge process.

REVIEW KNOWLEDGE REQUIREMENTS

Reuse of specialist knowledge that is of technical nature is closely tied to the PRINCE2 process of managing product delivery. In contrast, reuse of project management knowledge is standardized by any type of methodological approach – as to direct in the form of guidance method-wise – combined with and complemented by ProwLO. With the support of a project knowledge manager, the project management environment is tailored in such a way that knowledge reuse becomes natural for project managers. For specialist knowledge, accept a work package triggers 'Review of knowledge requirements'. This is an informal activity by definition, performed by specialists and monitored by the Project Manager. A knowledge requirement is simply a statement of a knowledge need required to deliver one or more products as defined by a Work Package. In case of a knowledge need with reuse potential, the Project Knowledge Manager may update the conceptual knowledge needs in the Knowledge Portal, including adding the meta-data (which is extensive by default). So the Project Knowledge Manager takes an observational role and looks for reuse potential associated with knowledge enquiries.

CAPTURE AD HOC KNOWLEDGE NEEDS

Execute a Work Package triggers 'Capture ad hoc knowledge needs'. Unlike the previous ProwLO activity, this is a formal procedure. The difference is that the Project Knowledge Manager is now held accountable for capture of emerging knowledge needs and needs to document findings, unlike the first activity in which he or she takes a more passive role as to observe how specialists deal with knowledge requirements under supervision of team managers. Different knowledge needs have different priorities. The Project Knowledge Manager should acknowledge this and act accordingly. Based on new findings, the conceptual knowledge needs for the project are updated. And later in the process, if these knowledge needs are generic across projects, Knowledge Value chains, if applicable, are updated as well (see 'Update Knowledge Value Chains').

EVALUATE SPECIALIST KNOWLEDGE REUSE

Deliver a Work Package triggers 'Evaluate Specialist Knowledge Reuse'. For specialists, this is a voluntary activity; for the Project Knowledge Manager, it is obligatory. The latter provides a trigger for the corresponding activity in Live Capture, and therefore data should be collected during managing product delivery and processed at the *final* Work Package of Controlling a Stage. It is important to keep in mind that the Project Knowledge Manager should take a proactive role in order to gather relevant data, simply by enquiry. If analysis shows a lack of knowledge reuse, potentially indicating other knowledge management problems, action should be taken. In case the problem is simply lack of knowledge at organizational level, then knowledge development is the only solution. Alternatively, if the knowledge is present but not reused efficiently and effectively, or reused at all, then additional measures need to be considered as to close knowledge and experience gaps, ranging from specific knowledge transfer acts to more profound organizational interventions at strategic and tactical level. Such knowledge gap analysis is arguably better performed in the context of Communities of Practice, outside the scope of ProwLO. Evaluate specialist knowledge reuse may result in 'Trigger/Endorse Specialist Knowledge Evaluation', associated with the knowledge needs in question, in the context of CoP. The latter process activity not only enables planned discovery of knowledge gaps, but also supports evolution of existing knowledge. Project Managers, on the other hand, do not need such specific method-wise triggers calling for assistance from the community, in any project-based process as knowledge *evaluation* activity is already covered by the KM activity plan, which is maintained throughout the project. Moreover, project managers can rely on direct knowledge support from the project management office (mostly present in project-based organizations), project knowledge manager and, not to forget, Project Board members. Notwithstanding, project managers can always ask fellow colleagues for advice. ProwLO recommends evaluation of management knowledge at the organizational level, potentially triggered by emerging knowledge needs, to be carried out by the project management office, which may evolve into an 'expertise centre' for the specific domain of project and programme management.

TRIGGER/ENDORSE SPECIALIST KNOWLEDGE EVALUATION

The specific trigger for evaluation of specific knowledge needs varies. As mentioned above, either knowledge evaluation is directed towards determining knowledge gaps, followed by knowledge development, or is concerned with modification of existing knowledge enabling its evolution. For specialist knowledge, it is paramount that such evaluation takes place in the context of the respective Communities of Practice. The project management office is not suited for this type of knowledge activity because of limited scope and expertise. It is not a 'command centre', like in the military, responsible for every type of operation in projects. The discipline experts, so much needed for their input, are rather dispersed and assigned to different projects. They are not part of a formal body like the PMO. Based on the multidisciplinary character of projects and inevitable interdependencies, engagement of experts from different fields may be necessary. Even project managers may join the discussion, depending on the issue and subject matter.

The Project Knowledge Manager is not necessarily the person who triggers this process of knowledge evaluation setting it in motion. Instead, he/she can provide a simple endorsement (online or in real person) that can be picked by subject matter experts. The latter knowledge authorities know best how to organize CoP engagement necessary for knowledge evaluation. It should be stressed that there are no formal roles in CoP. Instead, authority relationships in CoP emerge through interaction around expertise (Lesser & Storck, 2001). As CoP are an intricate web of personal relations of people who know and trust each other, it is not always straightforward for Project Knowledge Managers to initiate new learning. Once a CoP takes over and triggers and arranges knowledge evaluation, the concept of knowledge value chain takes a new level, transcending project boundaries, thanks to value-adding activities in social networks of experts. Web technology, ideally a knowledge portal, may facilitate the events required for knowledge evaluation; for example, to find evidence of knowledge gaps or to endorse knowledge evaluation online on the local intranet.

UPDATE ORGANIZATIONAL KNOWLEDGE BASE

Particular knowledge activities, triggered by CoP evaluation, may lead to an update of the organizational knowledge base, a follow-up activity. ProwLO recommends a centralized knowledgebase in which updating knowledge objects is the sole responsibility of the Project Knowledge Manager. So it is essential that the outcome of the previous activity, evaluation of specialist knowledge, includes feedback to the Project Knowledge Manager.

UPDATE KNOWLEDGE VALUE CHAINS

In conjunction with updating the knowledge base by adding/updating specific knowledge objects based on evident knowledge needs, the

Project Knowledge Manager is also responsible for updating the associated knowledge value chains. If the identified knowledge need is new, then a new value chain entity has to be created. This applies to emergent knowledge needs in particular, but also to earlier identified knowledge needs not yet backed by value chains that are considered as significant to be captured as chain entities. In other cases, knowledge evaluation may lead to updating existing knowledge value chains following modification of associated knowledge objects, as performed in the previously described activity. Just like other activities in the process, these two final activities focus on specialist, not management, knowledge. The other (prescribed) opportunity for updating *both* knowledge objects and knowledge value chains, but now for any type of knowledge, is during 'Optimize Knowledge Value chains' near the end of the project, described in the next chapter. Recall that knowledge value chains are also maintained (updating and creating) during each stage transition in the context of 'Trigger Knowledge Value Chains' (see Chapter 6).

IMPLICATIONS FOR OTHER FRAMEWORKS

Table 16 relates Reuse Specialist Knowledge with the Praxis Framework, PMBok and the ARCADIS process model.

Table 16 Reuse Specialist Knowledge Implications for Other Frameworks

PRINCE2 activity with ProwLO interface	Framework	Corresponding process element of alternative framework
Accept a Work Package	Praxis	Accept work package
	PMBoK	Workflow based on work packages is not an element of any process group. Work packages are merely addressed in the context of creating a Work Breakdown Structure (note that in PRINCE2, the focus is on products, not activities, typically associated with work)

(Continued)

Table 16 (Cont.)

PRINCE2 activity with ProwLO interface	Framework	Corresponding process element of alternative framework
	ARCADIS	Managing Product Delivery corresponds with the process of Project Execution (Advice, Design and Engineering), but is not formally embedded. Work is, however, organized in work packages, as this is also what the customer and internal systems require
Execute a Work Package	Praxis	Perform work
	PMBoK	This specialist activity is not addressed by PMBoK. As a result, additional control mechanisms – interesting from a project management perspective – cannot be covered. In PRINCE2, executing a work package does not confine to specialist work only. For example, the Team Manager, who monitors delivery closely, is responsible for the creation of Checkpoint reports
	ARCADIS	Is an obvious process, part of project execution
Deliver a Work Package	Praxis	Deliver products
	PMBoK	Handling of work packages is not covered by PMBoK
	ARCADIS	Handling of work packages is automated and aligned with an internal IT system

SUGGESTED ROLES AND RESPONSIBILITIES

Table 17 relates roles to activities in Reuse Specialist Knowledge.

Table 17 Reuse Specialist Knowledge Suggested Roles and Responsibilities

Activity/Role	Project Knowledge Manager	Project Manager	Project Board	1. Project Team Members 2. Chief Knowledge Officer 3. PMO
Review Knowledge Requirements	Updates knowledge needs	Reviewed by a Team Manager role concerning with product delivery, if part of the project organization. Possibly the same person as the Project Manager	–	–
Capture ad hoc Knowledge Needs	Capture on ad hoc basis by engaging with specialists in the team	Get informed	–	1. Update the Project Knowledge Manager voluntarily on individual needs
Evaluate Specialist Knowledge Reuse	Evaluate Document somewhere	Review	Reader	–
Trigger/ Endorse Specialist Knowledge Evaluation	Trigger, endorse. Communicate initiative to Project Manager	Be up-to-date	–	1. Execute knowledge evaluation activity in the context of Communities of Practice
Update Organizational Knowledgebase	Update using an IT tool	Alerted	–	3. Alerted
Update Knowledge Value Chains	Update	Review	Reader	–

9 Optimize knowledge value chains

Optimize Knowledge Value Chains (see Figure 17) runs in parallel with Closing a Project. The main objective of this process is to consolidate altered knowledge value chains applied in the project. What follows is modification of knowledge objects mapped to these entities, but also modification of knowledge objects without backing of value chains. The added value of creating new value chain entities for existing knowledge objects, sometimes legacy files, is rationalization of the added value of knowledge needs satisfaction (the supply of content or access to knowledge). Not only based on statement of the added value itself but also, with the right tool, based on measurement of knowledge processes dealing with the knowledge objects in question (based on simple metrics). Therefore, measuring knowledge processes is not an end in itself, but supports the continuation of adding value processes centred around a valid knowledge need. When such a claim of validity no longer holds, then the knowledge value chain should be discontinued and archived, while access to specific knowledge objects supporting the need should be restricted, provided that these objects have limited value in general (i.e. limited reuse potential in different context). Accordingly, such knowledge objects could be designated by labels such as 'not up-to-date' – fostering caution in knowledge application and reuse or become simply removed from the central knowledge base. A notable feature of Optimize Knowledge Value Chains is the attention to story telling. Projects are vehicles of learning and newly gained experience should be examined for creation of stories.

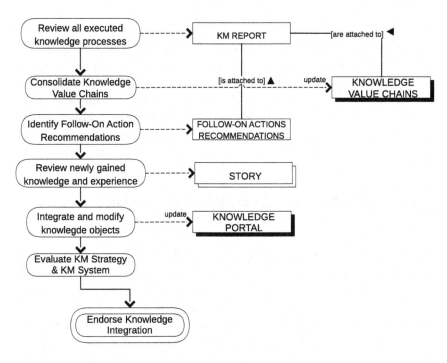

Figure 17 Optimize Knowledge Value Chains.

REVIEW ALL EXECUTED KNOWLEDGE PROCESSES

The first activity is to 'Review all executed knowledge processes'. Based on the generic knowledge value chain (see Chapter 3, Figure 5), there are different categories of knowledge processes which can be used as a starting point in evaluation. The majority of knowledge processes that occurred in the project, in hindsight near project end, is covered by the KM activity plan which is used as input. This review activity should also consider undocumented KM activities that were performed on the fly (often in ad hoc fashion) without any reference in the KM activity Plan or Project Plan, the second input document. In many cases, knowledge application activities – which are by definition task-centric and directly related to project output – are recorded in the Project Plan but not identified as a distinct knowledge process. The output of this review process is a KM Report. The KM Report has two key functions. First, it supports the notion of Knowledge Value Chains as a management tool. Activities referenced or defined in the Report provide evidence of chain activity that can be traced to unique projects and measured in time and resources spent. Together with measurement of *online* knowledge processes captured by a knowledge portal (or advanced knowledge base), this makes Knowledge Value Chains really quantifiable. The single KM report is attached to all knowledge value chain entities affected. The second function of the Report is to be used as input for 'Endorse knowledge integration' by the Project Board as part of the activity 'Authorize Project Closure' in the context of directing a project. Essentially, this is *selective* continuation of value-adding activity inherent to knowledge value chains.

CONSOLIDATE KNOWLEDGE VALUE CHAINS

Consolidate Knowledge Value Chains update all knowledge value chains relevant to the project, in line with the primary objective of the main process (optimization). Every element of the chain is reviewed thoroughly and updated if necessary. One of these elements, the list of related KM activities, follows from previous entries and/or 'Review all executed knowledge processes'. Combined with the KM Report, consolidated knowledge value chains enable strategic positioning of knowledge, a follow-up capability. While individual value chains stress the strategic value of knowledge at object level, a broader perspective enables to prioritize specific knowledge needs over others. Such prioritization approach directly affects the knowledge value chain element of integration push and pull strategies after project completion/end. For example, by prioritising knowledge value chains based on aggregated information, a more aggressive strategy can be applied in terms of knowledge push. A priority list also helps to define or set preference of specific strategies as to foster knowledge pull, leading to greater knowledge satisfaction. Although integration strategies should be aligned with corporate KM strategy, this does not imply that multiple strategies are not permitted or that individual knowledge value chains may not deviate from corporate policy. Exceptions, following knowledge value chain implications, should be possible based on principle of tailoring.

IDENTIFY FOLLOW-ON ACTION RECOMMENDATIONS

'Identify Follow-On Action Recommendations' is a parallel PRINCE2 *concept* only now with a focus on knowledge management. Follow-on actions may include knowledge management activities after project closure, i.e. knowledge processing activities in line with knowledge value chains. Second, based on lessons learned on the application of ProwLO, follow-on actions may include practical recommendations on how to effectively apply ProwLO in future projects. This may involve scaling the method. Tailoring of the process model is not recommended. Tailoring standard templates – a typical outcome of knowledge evaluation – used for ProwLO, on the other hand, should be very limited because of fixed data formats. Typically, scaling focuses on formality. ProwLO process activities can be performed formally or informally. The difference is in how data is captured and exchanged, enabled by means of communications and IT which may vary. Like in PRINCE2, it could be possible to replace formal documents with informal communication. In order to prevent the PINO version of ProwLO (ProwLO in Name Only), all ProwLO activities, and thus, all processes in their entirety, should be performed. A standard follow-on action is to evaluate the KM strategy and KM system, the final ProwLO activity of Optimize Knowledge Value Chains. Once defined, the follow-on action recommendations are added to the KM Report.

REVIEW NEWLY GAINED KNOWLEDGE AND EXPERIENCE

The purpose of 'Review newly gained knowledge and experience' is to create one or more Stories on knowledge development and knowledge capture and relate them to project success or general increase in organizational capability. With regard to experience, Stories complement the standardized knowledge objects of Cases and Lessons Learned, discussed earlier. Stories are a very creative way to counter project amnesia and an increasing number of organizations are using story telling for organizational memory. Potentially, Stories can hold more contextual information, but are still compressed, and are therefore well suited to deal with the tacit dimensions of experience. The Project Knowledge Manager, who is assigned responsibility for this task, has to be a good listener (for gathering data) but also he or she should also be able to connect the dots of a story line in a very appealing way. Stories can be either documented or recorded as rich media and are not bound by a rigid, standard format (like Cases and Lessons Learned as imposed by standardized processes). Alternatively, this activity could be outsourced to a project external Consultant (as an example of scaling). Specialized consultants may be better equipped to deal with the unconventional aspect of Stories and are arguably better skilled in story telling, a key requisite.

INTEGRATE AND MODIFY KNOWLEDGE OBJECTS

'Integrate and modify knowledge objects' is essentially an update process. All newly created knowledge objects need to be uploaded either to a central corporate knowledge base or to a more advanced knowledge portal so as to enable knowledge integration. The same applies to all modified knowledge objects, based on the principle of knowledge evolution. The justification for knowledge integration of these objects is potentially provided by associated knowledge value chains applied during the project. The integration process that follows uploading and updating knowledge objects depends strongly on proprietary software. In order to deal with information overload, software tools need clever solutions. The most obvious approach is extensive use of meta-data for better search capability.

EVALUATE THE KM STRATEGY AND KM SYSTEM

The final activity of Optimization of Knowledge Value Chains is 'Evaluate KM Strategy and KM System'. Optimization, or put simply, getting the most out of knowledge processing and consequently business processing (i.e. knowledge application), requires an effective KM strategy and KM system (not just IT system), aligned with ProwLO. Assuming that ProwLO is state-of-the-art and fully in service of optimized project, programme and portfolio management, daily practice in organizations may not be supportive to achieve this level of excellence. Maturity research shows that there are no organizations with a maturity level optimized across all organizational dimensions (if any at all). Currently, the most mature organizations have at most a repeated process (level 2), backed by some level of defined process (level 3) inspired by the best practice guidance in the form of process assets, sometimes process protocols. Even if ProwLO is top-down supported, alignment with the rest of an organization remains challenging, to say, at least. In particular, the people and culture dimension forms a major obstacle. Note that learning organizations are not commonplace. Therefore, successful implementation of ProwLO is also a case of change management and maturing the organization is paramount. So, besides alignment with the KM strategy and KM system, the effectiveness of

ProwLO also depends on organizational maturity and overall organizational alignment (across different organizational dimensions and/or functions). Assuming that projects (or programmes) can be vehicles of change, ProwLO-driven projects should be able to define recommendations for such change. The ProwLO recommendations, however, should be limited to evaluation of the KM strategy and KM system, not necessarily captured in a formal report. The general project recommendations (according to the project management methodology) may take a greater scope as to safeguard organizational alignment, for example, in future projects. The change recommendations are primarily targeted at the chief officer concerned with Knowledge Management, but also internal Project Board members with senior titles, and thus, authority necessary to promote change. The end of 'Evaluate KM Strategy and KM System' triggers 'Endorse Knowledge Integration' by the Project Board in the context of Directing Knowledge Processes.

IMPLICATIONS FOR OTHER FRAMEWORKS

There are no specific interfaces with PRINCE2 activities as part of Closing Project. This implies that the work by Project Knowledge Manager related to 'Optimize Knowledge Value Chains' can be performed independently, yet in the same time-frame.

SUGGESTED ROLES AND RESPONSIBILITIES

Table 18 relates roles to activities in Optimize Knowledge Value Chains.

Table 18 Optimize Knowledge Value Chains Suggested Roles and Responsibilities

Activity/Role	Project Knowledge Manager	Project Manager	Project Board	1. Project Team Members 2. Chief Knowledge Officer 3. PMO
Review all Executed Knowledge Processes	Produce KM Report	Review report	Review report	2. Review 3. Review

(*Continued*)

Table 18 (Cont.)

Activity/Role	Project Knowledge Manager	Project Manager	Project Board	1. Project Team Members 2. Chief Knowledge Officer 3. PMO
Consolidate Knowledge Value Chains	Update knowledge value chain entities	Review	Reader	2. Review 3. Review
Identify Follow-On Action Recommendations	Define	Approve	Review	2. Contemplate, implement yes or no 3. Support
Review newly gained Knowledge and Experience	Produce or facilitate capture of Stories if performed by (external) Consultant	Review	Reader	3. Foster knowledge integration
Integrate and Modify Knowledge Objects	Knowledge integration	–	–	3. Informed by Project Knowledge Manager on new updates
Evaluate KM Strategy and KM System	Evaluate Document somewhere Inform Chief Knowledge Officer of analysis	Reader	Reader	2. Review

10 Post-project knowledge control

As follows from Chapter 2, section 'A Parallel Process Model to Project Management', post-project knowledge control (see Figure 18) is not part of the project management environment (i.e. scope of the single performing project). It can be triggered by new projects but the process itself has little in common with the project life cycle itself, which provides the foundation of any project management approach and framework, and that of ProwLO (a key premise elaborated in Chapter 2). Accordingly, the best way to address this final ProwLO process is as ProwLO+. The very existence of this process signifies that the lifecycle of knowledge transcends

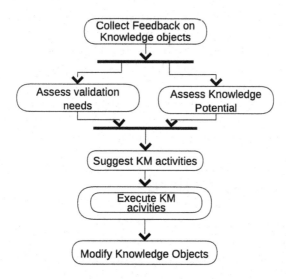

Figure 18 Post-Project Knowledge Control.

conventional projects and needs additional effort for its continuous evolution. Besides new projects, the second trigger is events taking place in the context of Communities of Practice, particularly knowledge evaluation processes. The key thing here is to link feedback of CoP with the centralized function responsible for knowledge control, including content management in the event of updating relevant knowledge objects.

COLLECT FEEDBACK ON KNOWLEDGE OBJECTS

The first post-project knowledge control activity is 'Collect feedback on knowledge objects'. Knowledge users generally do not interact with knowledge value chains but the objects related to them. Collecting feedback of knowledge objects helps to position the associated knowledge value chain, in business value for example, or reuse potential. Not of less importance, the quality of the knowledge object can be improved. The activity depends on the use of a central knowledge repository for both knowledge integration and collecting feedback, assuming a web-based solution with feedback options. Setting up such centralized solution greatly reduces the problem of difficulty finding the right knowledge (as compared to a decentralized approach leading to fragmentation). The additional feedback capability, on the other hand, fosters knowledge evaluation and supports online collection of feedback. Difficulty in finding the right knowledge, however, is a multi-faceted problem. Web-based access not necessarily solves the issue of poor accessibility of artefacts. For example, in the light of usability engineering, system design may not be user-friendly. Also, the search function may not meet user expectations. Furthermore, due to different root causes, the centrally available knowledge may not be up-to-date. Post-project knowledge control should deal with these types of problems for effective and efficient feedback on existing knowledge objects.

ASSESS VALIDATION NEEDS

Following collecting feedback, there are two parallel activities, namely, 'Assess validation needs' and 'Assess knowledge potential'. The former is triggered by analysis of new feedback that indicates validity issues. For example, a suggested Template centrally available could be out-of-date, either significantly tailored when applied in practice or replaced by a newer standard (e.g. reflecting changes in the overall methodology, corporate wide). If a validity issue is discovered, then the current state of the knowledge object, in terms of content and knowledge need meta-data, needs to be readdressed. Combined with assessment of knowledge potential, the knowledge control responsible function and role can then suggest follow-up KM activities.

ASSESS KNOWLEDGE POTENTIAL

Assessment of knowledge potential is an essential element of post-project knowledge control because it directly links knowledge objects to knowledge value chains with all their attributes. Recall that Knowledge Value Chains are a tool to assess the business value of knowledge. The information they provide makes it a lot easier to interpret the value of specific objects associated with these entities. The greater the value of the knowledge value chain, the more significant the role of the knowledge object supporting the knowledge need linked with a particular knowledge value chain. It should be stressed that this activity focuses on knowledge *potential*, not current value, and thus requires some level projection combined with raw data based on current trends. Based on estimation of the knowledge potential knowledge needs, KM activities can be prioritised. Do not forget that the knowledge control function may trigger activities outside the regular planning scope of projects. Therefore, resources and time should be spent wisely.

SUGGEST KM ACTIVITIES

'Suggest KM Activities' may relate to the various knowledge processes engaging with the knowledge need in question (based on the knowledge life cycle presented in Chapter 3, section 'Define and Plan Knowledge Activities') – all in order to satisfy a knowledge need at organizational level, or at least with organizational relevance. The key proposition here is that developed knowledge objects *contribute* to knowledge needs satisfaction. Hence, the suggested KM activities should primarily focus on codified knowledge, which makes post-project knowledge control tangible, providing a clear starting point: evolution of codified knowledge. On the other hand, in case there is a strong tacit dimension to the knowledge need involved, a focus on skills over declarative knowledge (also known as 'know-what'), then knowledge integration may require socialization processes (recall tacit-to-tacit conversion) as well. Therefore, various types of KM activities should be taken into account. It should be stressed that knowledge is principally fallible (with exceptions like scientific statement with scientific proofs or common truths of the physical world, including the world of physics). Based on this awareness, the outcome of a KM activity may trigger a dispute of a knowledge claim (the claim associated with an object, providing intrinsic value), or even worse, consensus that the knowledge claim no longer holds. In either case, the knowledge object loses status and the associated knowledge value chain either loses (measurable) value, or needs to evolve – provided that it still relates to an active knowledge need, or devolve (e.g. narrowing its applicability, setting a more realistic knowledge potential). Note that evolution could be simply the replacement of a knowledge object that does meet validity criteria. This also means that knowledge value chains themselves can lose purpose and become obsolete. Finally, validity does not equal true or false. There is also a gray area in between that may require a scale like the one used according to the Cases-method of Chapter 5 for external validity. So, the concept of knowledge validity also refers to the generic quality of knowledge (its applicability in different but similar contexts). Adequate testing of knowledge validity, in line with the principle of evolution, should be fostered and planned as part of evaluation activities.

EXECUTE KM ACTIVITIES

Following suggestion of specific KM activities targeting knowledge objects driven by knowledge needs and managed according to knowledge value chains, execution of activities is the next process activity. Based on priority, the activities are executed, and in the right context. Rather than straightforward, there are a few side aspects. The decision whether to execute particular activities or not is made based on mutual agreement between the experts and the central function for knowledge control. A recommendation is that experts and key actors assigned to the suggested KM activities should have the final say. This particularly holds for cases, the majority, where the context for performing KM activities corresponds to Communities of Practice. That is, experts gather and make a joint effort directed towards simple goals, dealing with any issues. The central function should be aware that in CoP, relations are formed based on expertise instead of formal roles. So in order get things done, an open and cooperative attitude is required, in which dialogue and discussion prevails instead of simple commanding based on quasi authorities institutionalized to progress knowledge management. Another interesting context is concurrent or future projects as part of a greater portfolio (not the original project, as being source of particular knowledge and closed already). Advanced portfolio planning – management across projects – could potentially incorporate KM activities based on knowledge relevancy and foresight (e.g. rooted in project similarity). The latter, however, is not commonplace. A more common context is the Project Management Office as expertise centre for project management. In the case of the latter, planned KM activities can be executed on the fly, especially when the PMO is the same body responsible for post-project knowledge control.

MODIFY KNOWLEDGE OBJECTS

The final activity of post-project knowledge control (and ProwLO process model) is 'Modify knowledge objects'. This is a straightforward update procedure, utilizing the functionality of a corporate knowledge base or advanced knowledge portal. If necessary, the associated knowledge value chains are updated as well as to reflect changes and knowledge implications. It is beyond the scope of this book and manual to elaborate on software functions but it makes sense to implement version control in order to enable continuous improvement of knowledge artefacts. Notwithstanding, ProwLO is the first methodology in the business of best practice guidance with a strong Technology component. In fact, some activities are simply not possible, effective and/or efficiently performed without software tools. Although the data models behind the processes are now in the public domain, thanks to publishing, incorporating them in software is subject to licensing and copyright law. This, for example, applies to the Cases-method. The application of ProwLO with or without reproduction of copyright material should be fostered even if new IT investment is necessary. The (measurable) benefits of a controlled project knowledge management environment – aligned with projects – outweigh the costs, including costs related to change management. To mention a few, the benefit of knowledge needs satisfaction is a game changer, leading to greater employee satisfaction, better productivity, empowerment, a sense of ownership, etc. For project-based organizations, only

ProwLO provides the tools and mindset for personal mastery at the individual level and enables optimized processes at the organizational level. In conclusion, complemented by advanced IT solutions for such practical tasks like updating knowledge objects, ProwLO can truly deliver learning with positive business outcomes (read as cause and effect). This is accomplished, for example, by a significant increase in knowledge reuse and closing knowledge gaps professionally. When learning does not translate into direct or indirect benefits, then something must have gone wrong: learning should always add value to business. So, learning outcomes (as a given) do not necessarily equal outcomes of learning in terms of business impact. ProwLO takes care of both.

IMPLICATIONS FOR OTHER FRAMEWORKS

Post-project knowledge control, unrelated to any project management process, has no impact on any project management framework in terms of process adjustments. This process complements any process model based on a project's life cycle.

SUGGESTED ROLES AND RESPONSIBILITIES

Table 19 relates roles to activities in Post-Project Knowledge Control.

Table 19 Post-Project Knowledge Control Suggested Roles and Responsibilities

Activity/ Role	Project Knowledge Manager	Project Manager	Project Board	1. Project Team Members 2. Chief Knowledge Officer 3. PMO
Collect Feedback on	Knowledge foraging* and knowledge pull in	Provide feedback on PM	Provided with access to the	2. Implement organizational policy in order to institutionalize

(*Continued*)

Table 19 (Cont.)

Activity/ Role	Project Knowledge Manager	Project Manager	Project Board	1. Project Team Members 2. Chief Knowledge Officer 3. PMO
Knowledge Objects	general. Networking with a focus	knowledge artefacts	knowledge base	feedback to the Project Knowledge Manager
Assess Validation Needs	Evaluate knowledge claim, quality of knowledge, external validity.** If applicable, invite knowledge owners to assess validity	Endorse validation needs	–	1. Individuals may get an invitation to perform validation
Assess Knowledge Potential	Contemplate, estimate value	Review as member of the PM Community of Practice	–	1. Provide specialist input if necessary
Suggest KM Activities	Make suggestions	–	–	2. Approve/ Endorse
Execute KM Activities	Facilitate and support	Potentially participate	–	1. Potentially participate
Modify Knowledge Objects	Knowledge modification and knowledge integration	–	–	3. Support knowledge integration, e.g. using social networks

* Coined by Jenkin (2013).
** External validity refers to how generic the knowledge claim is, or how generic applicable and context-specific a knowledge object is.

Appendix I: KM system analysis

Table 20 provides the results of a KM system analysis at Tebodin, an international engineering company. Table 21 provides the results of a KM system analysis at ARCADIS, a Dutch-international engineering company.

Table 20 KM system analysis at Tebodin (Company X)

Conceptual Knowledge Need	KM process	Role of Prince2	KM mechanism/ technology	Current situation in Tebodin
Lessons Learned (LL)	Knowledge capture	Issue Log, Lessons Learned Log, Lessons Learned Report, Review the Stage status	Project reviews, Live capture	- Project reviews in limited use and only at the end the project (no intermediate 'Gate Reviews') - Live capture (instant capture and documentation of knowledge when something new is learned) lacks completely - Use of Issue Logs is unknown

(Continued)

Table 20 (Cont.)

Conceptual Knowledge Need	KM process	Role of Prince2	KM mechanism/ technology	Current situation in Tebodin
	Knowledge integration	Capture previous lessons	Web-based access	- Lessons Learned are captured and added to a best practice database, which is online available - Referring back to existing Lesson Learned is not a formalized routine (as prescribed by PRINCE2) - Lessons Learned do not contain contextual information (meta-data)
Cases	Knowledge capture	See LL	See LL + Cases-method	- See lessons learned above (similar approach to knowledge capture) - No procedure exists for capture of Project Management Cases; problems + solutions and related lessons learned are captured in 'free format', if captured at all - Cases do not contain contextual information (meta-data)

(Continued)

Table 20 (Cont.)

Conceptual Knowledge Need	KM process	Role of Prince2	KM mechanism/ technology	Current situation in Tebodin
	Knowledge integration	Capture previous lessons	Web-based access	- Cases are digitally available but are not classified as a specific type of knowledge object
	Knowledge application	–	Case-based reasoning	- Based on personal experiences or experiences from others which are shared ad hoc and informally through *personal* contact
Best practices	Knowledge integration	–	Web-based access	- Best practices are digitally available in the Lessons Learned database - There is no strong separation between best practices (generic knowledge) and lessons learned (more specific knowledge)
	Knowledge application	PSO, Project Approach, Select the Project Approach and assemble the Project Brief	Expertise centre, Routine in order embed BP, Standards Management Information System (MIS)	- For support in the application of best practices, one has to rely on colleagues - Project Management Offices only support bigger projects and usually do not have the required maturity level associated with an Expertise Centre.

(*Continued*)

Table 20 (Cont.)

Conceptual Knowledge Need	KM process	Role of Prince2	KM mechanism/ technology	Current situation in Tebodin
				- Every project has a Project Approach and it is based on best practices
				- Process descriptions only exist on paper (as part of the annual TQS manual updated every year)
				- The process model for project management is not based on a standard like PRINCE2
Templates	Knowledge integration	–	Web-based access	- Templates are digitally available
	Knowledge application	PSO	Expertise centre	- Templates are a safeguard for quality and are maintained by the Quality department
Tools	Knowledge integration	–	Web-based access	- Tools like manuals are digitally available, especially in SharePoint
	Knowledge application	PSO	Expertise centre	- For support in the application of Tools, one can count on Communities of Practice, referred to as 'the discipline'. In practice, one usually calls a colleague

(Continued)

Table 20 (Cont.)

Conceptual Knowledge Need	KM process	Role of Prince2	KM mechanism/ technology	Current situation in Tebodin
Examples	Knowledge integration	–	Web-based access	- Representative examples are digitally available - Specific examples like project documentation are less accessible (document management does not support distribution)
IntraKnotes	Knowledge integration	–	Web-based access	- Organization warns of the use of social media due to confidential information - For chat, one uses Microsoft lync - There is no twitter-based platform for exchange of short messages
All	Project-based learning	–	Project reviews, Cases-method	- Project reviews (evaluation) in limited use - No procedure for the capture of Project Management Cases
All	Knowledge evaluation/ evolution		Knowledge Portal	- There is no software that supports the entire lifecycle of knowledge with a consequence that the best practice database gets filled

(*Continued*)

Table 20 (Cont.)

Conceptual Knowledge Need	KM process	Role of Prince2	KM mechanism/ technology	Current situation in Tebodin
				with redundant information, information that is no longer up-to-date, or information that adds little value

Table 21 KM system Analysis at ARCADIS (Company Y)

Conceptual Knowledge need	KM process	Role of Prince2	KM mechanism/ technology	Situation in Company Y
Lessons Learned	Knowledge capture	Issue Log, Lessons Learned Log, Lessons Learned Report	Project reviews, Live capture	- Project Reviews in limited use - Complete lack of Live capture - Limited use of the Issue Log, LL Log and LL Report
	Knowledge integration	–	Web-based access	- Lessons Learned are digitally *not* available
Cases	Knowledge capture	See LL	See LL + Cases-method	- See Lessons Learned above - No procedure for capturing PM Cases
	Knowledge integration	–	Web-based access	- Cases are digitally *not* available
	Knowledge application	–	Case-based reasoning	- Based on personal experience or experiences from others which are shared ad hoc and informally through *personal* contact (Individualized-Personalization)

(*Continued*)

Table 21 (Cont.)

Conceptual Knowledge need	KM process	Role of Prince2	KM mechanism/ technology	Situation in Company Y
Best practices	Knowledge integration	–	Web-based access	- Best practices are digitally *not* available
	Knowledge application	PSO, Project Approach, – –	Expertise centre, Routine in order to embed Best Practices, Standards Management Information System (MIS)	- For support in the application of best practices, one has to rely on colleagues - The Project Approach is a little too limited with regard to content - In the Project Approach, there is also little reference to best practices - The process model in the MIS is not based on a standard (PRINCE2 for PM)
Templates	Knowledge integration	–	Web-based access	- Templates are digitally available but sometimes not up-to-date
	Knowledge application	PSO	Expertise centre	- For support in the application of Templates, one has to rely on colleagues
Tools	Knowledge integration	–	Web-based access	- Different Tools are digitally available, but this could be extended
	Knowledge application	PSO	Expertise centre	- For support in the application of tools, one has to rely on colleagues
Examples	Knowledge integration	–	Web-based access	- Only limited examples are digitally available; often they are exchanged in ad hoc fashion and informally (Individualized-Codification)

(*Continued*)

Table 21 (Cont.)

Conceptual Knowledge need	KM process	Role of Prince2	KM mechanism/ technology	Situation in Company Y
Alerts	Knowledge integration	–	Web-based access	- Alerts (in digital form) are completely lacking
All	Project-based learning	–	Project reviews, Cases-method	- Project reviews only in limited use - No procedure for capture of PM Cases

Appendix II: Case example

Table 22 provides a sample of a complex case.

Table 22 Case Example

Case title	*'Design phase of the life extension of an old naval support ship'.*
Identify the initial problem	Got behind schedule.
Identify the causes behind the problem	**Emergent factor(s):** There was a sudden change in regulations which required a significant change in the design requirement mid-project. **Situational aspects:** Very tight timescale.
Analyze management actions	**Corrective action(s):** 1) increased number of design engineers, and 2) moved to a three-shift system. **Expected outcome(s):** These actions will deal with the increase in work and increasing schedule slippage.
Evaluate project behaviour	**Actual outcome(s):** Delay in the detail of the design requirement being specified by the authorities.
Identify Lessons Learned	Cross-impacts should be forecasted; Cross-shift communications should be improved, etc.
Meta-data Domain	**Domain:** Project Management. **Knowledge areas:** Project Time Management; Project Integration Management.

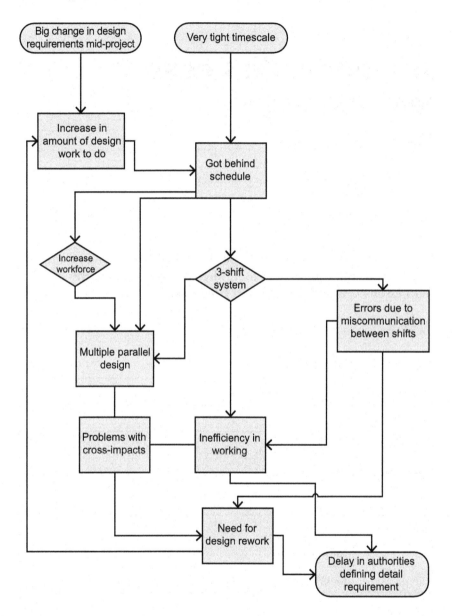

Figure 19 Causal Structure of a Case Example.

Appendix III: Lessons learned log

Table 23 provides the logical layout for a Lessons Learned Template required for the capture of Cases, whereas Table 24 captures remaining Lessons Learned (not derived from Cases).

1) Cases:

Table 23 Lessons Learned Log Template

Case number		
Case title		
Number of iterations	(for Example 2)	
Follow-on Actions		
Meta-data	Domain	
	Knowledge areas	
	External validity	
Iteration 1		
Problem analysis	Problem	
	Causes	**Emergent factors:** **Situational factors:**

(*Continued*)

Table 23 (Cont.)

Decisions and actions	Taken decision and/or actions	1) 2)
	Expected outcome	
	Comments regarding decision-making process	
'Project behaviour'	Eventual result	
	Evaluation of taken decision and/or actions	
Lessons Learned	1) 2)	
Iteration 2		
Problem analysis	Problem	(See eventual result of previous iteration)
	Causes	See project behaviour previous iteration
Decision and actions	Taken decision and/or actions	1) 2)
	Expected outcome	
	Comments regarding decision-making process	
'Project behaviour'	Eventual result	
	Evaluation of taken decision and/or actions	
Lessons Learned	1) 2)	

2) Remaining Lessons Learned:

Table 24 Lessons Learned Log Section Lessons Learned

Lesson number		
Lesson		
Follow-on actions		
Meta-data	*Domain*	
	Knowledge areas	
	External validity	

Appendix IV: Meta-models

EVOLUTION OF PRINCE2 (2005 EDITION) TO PRINCE2 2017 UPDATE, META MODEL ANALYSIS

Since the PRINCE2 2005 edition, PRINCE2 has been updated twice: in 2009 and 2017. Both updates are considered as evolutionary steps. This means that the structure of the original method has persisted to some extent over time. If we compare the meta-models of the 2005 and 2017 editions (see Figures 20 and 21), we see that specific elements of the method have remained largely consistent, including the concepts of 'process', 'activity', 'product' and 'role'. In Figure 21, these process elements are coloured black. Combined, these four concepts form the foundation of the PRINCE2 process model. The concept of Technique as a distinct element was omitted in the 2009 Update, partly being absorbed by the Themes aspect, but the 2017 Update reintroduced Techniques by linking them with Themes. In 2009, the concept of Component was replaced by Theme, and this approach did not change in the 2017 update. Since 2009, the method places great emphasis on Principles, and, therefore, are included in the later meta-model. As a concept, principles have an indirect relationship with the process model. The need for tailoring PRINCE2 has first led to a new chapter on Tailoring in the 2009 update. In the 2017 version, besides a key focus on the separate chapters of 'Tailoring and adopting PRINCE2' and to a lesser extent 'Considerations for organizational adoption', tailoring is addressed as a key aspect of every process and theme, in the corresponding chapters, adding tailoring guidelines. This new approach has led to the notion of 'tailoring requirements', which align the method with specific project needs. The new activity of 'Agree

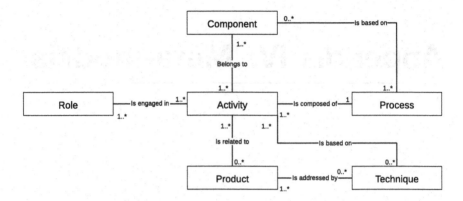

Figure 20 PRINCE2 2005 Meta-Model.

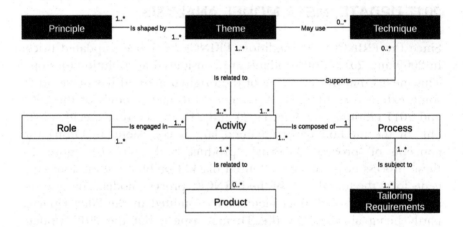

Figure 21 PRINCE2 2017 Update Meta-Model.

tailoring requirements' as part of Initiating a Project ensures that such tailoring requirements become part of the project approach.

META-MODEL OF ProwLO

A meta-model of ProwLO is depicted in Figure 22. Essentially, ProwLO consists of 8 processes consisting of multiple management activities, i.e. ProwLO sub-processes. As a whole, these processes cover knowledge needs, which drive knowledge processes. Knowledge processes in turn may trigger management activities and are supported by knowledge

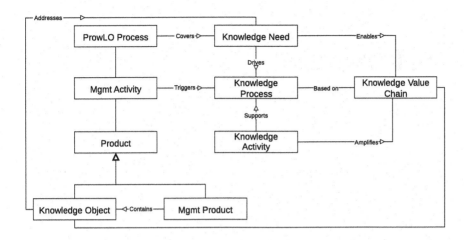

Figure 22 ProwLO Meta-Model.

activities (possibly defined in the KM activity plan). Every management activity may deal with specific products, either management products, including ProwLO external project management information (e.g. the PRINCE2 PID) and newly defined ProwLO products (e.g. the KM activity plan), or knowledge objects (which are based on and address reusable knowledge needs). A key concept of ProwLO is the Knowledge Value Chain. This Knowledge Value Chain provides the foundation for well-defined knowledge processes, is enabled by identifiable knowledge needs, potentially captured, thanks to ProwLO, and amplified by knowledge activities, increasing the value of specific knowledge types, in particular thanks to codified knowledge objects for greater knowledge integration.

References

Archibald, R.D. (2004). State of the art in project management: 2004. *PMI-Sao Paulo 4th International Seminar on Project Management, Sao Paulo, Brazil, Dec. 9–10 2004.*

Barnes, M. (2002). A long term view of project management – its past and its likely future. Retrieved June 25, 2007, from www.pmforum.org/library/papers/2002/longtermpmbarnes.pdf.

Becerra-Fernandez, I., Gonzalez, A., & Sabherwal, R. (2004). *Knowledge Management Challenges, Solutions, and Technologies.* New York: Prentice Hall.

Boh, W. (2007). Mechanisms for sharing knowledge in project-based organizations. *Information and Organization, 17* (1), 27–58.

Chen, F., Romano, N.C., Jr., Nunamaker, J., Jr., & Briggs, R. (2003). A collaborative project management architecture. In *Hicss '03: Proceedings of the 36th Annual Hawaii International Conference on System Sciences (hicss'03) – track1* (p. 15.1). Washington, DC: IEEE Computer Society.

Clark, D. (2004). After action reviews. Retrieved December 18, 2007, from www.nwlink.com/~Donclark/leader/leadaar.html.

Collinson, C. (2005, February 1). Knowledge management – learning whilst doing – facilitating an after action review. *EzineArticles.* Retrieved March 01, 2008, from http://ezinearticles.com/?Knowledge-Management—Learning-Whilst-Doing—Facilitating-an-After-Action-Review&id=12447.

Cook, S., & Brown, J. (1999). Bridging epistemologies: the generative dance between organizational knowledge and organizational knowing. *Organization Science, 10* (4), 381–400.

Damm, D., & Schindler, M. (2002). Security issues of a knowledge medium for distributed project work. *International Journal of Project Management, 20* (1), 37–47.

Eden, C., Williams, T., Ackermann, F., & Howick, S. (2000). The role of feedback dynamics in disruption and delay on the nature of Disruption and Delay (D&D) in major projects. *The Journal of the Operational Research Society, 51* (3), 291–300.

Edwards, P. (Ed.). (1967). *The Encyclopedia of Philosophy.* New York: Macmillan Publishing Co.

Fong, P., & Yip, J. (2006). An investigative study of the application of lessons learned systems in construction projects. *Journal for Education in the Built Environment, 1* (2), 27–38.

Gasik, S. (2011). Chapter 13. Project knowledge management. Retrieved April 1, 2011, from www.sybena.pl/dokumenty/PMBoK-project-knowledge-management-area-Gasik.pdf.

Hansen, M., Nohria, N., & Tierney, T. (1999). Whats your strategy for managing knowledge? *Harvard Business Review, 77* (2), 106–116.

Hemsley Fraser Group Limited. (2017). Retrieved February 7, 2018, from www.hemsleyfraser.co.uk.

Hirschhorn, L. (1997). *Reworking Authority: Leading and Following in the Post-Modern Organization.* Cambridge, MA: MIT Press.

Hofer-Alfeis, J., & van der Spek, R. (2002). The knowledge strategy process – an instrument for business owners. In T.H. Davenport & G.J.B. Probst (Eds.), *Knowledge Management Case Book.* Weinheim: John Wiley & Sons, pp. 24–39.

Huber, G. (1991). Organizational learning: the contributing processes and the literature. *Organizational Science, 2* (1), 88–115.

Jenkin, T.A. (2013). Extending the 4I Organizational Learning Model: information sources, foraging processes and tools. *Administrative Sciences, 3,* 96–109.

Joshi, K. (2001). A framework to study knowledge management behaviors during decision making. In *Proceedings of the 34th Annual Hawaii International Conference on Systemsciences (hicss-34) (Vol. 4).*

Larsen, K.R., & Eargle, D. (Eds.) (2015). Theories used in IS research wiki. Retrieved February 4, 2018, from https://is.theorizeit.org/wiki/Organizational_knowledge_creation.

Lesser, E.L., & Storck, J. (2001). Communities of practice and organizational performance. *IBM Systems Journal, 40* (4), 831–841.

Litten, D. (2017). PRINCE2 2017 give ad hoc direction. Retrieved February 4, 2018, from www.prince2primer.com/prince2-2017-give-ad-hoc-direction.

Loch, I., & Morris, P. (2003). Organisational learning and knowledge creation in project-based organisations. Retrieved June 25, 2007, from www.bartlett.ucl.ac.uk/research/management/OrganLearning.pdf.

Markus, L.A. (2001). Toward a theory of knowledge reuse: types of knowledge reuse-situations and factors in reuse success. *Journal of Management Information Systems, 18* (1), 57–93.

McElroy, M. (2003). *The New Knowledge Management – Complexity, Learning, and Sustainable Innovation.* New York: Butterworth Heinemann.

Milton, N. (2005). *Knowledge Management for Teams and Projects.* Oxford, UK: Chandos Publishing.

Newell, S., Laurent, S., Edelman, L., Scarbrough, H., Swan, J., & Bresnen, M. (2004). Sharing learning across projects: limits to current 'best practice' initiatives. In *5th European Conference on Organizational Knowledge.* Innsbruck, Austria.

Nonaka, I. (1994). A dynamic theory of organizational knowledge creation. *Organization Science, 5* (1), 14–37.

Onna, M., & Koning, A. (2002). *De Kleine Prince2, Gids Voor Projectmanagement.* Den Haag: TenHagen Stam Uitgevers.

Ribeiro, F. (2005). Using experience based cases to support construction business processes. In *Cib w78's 22nd International Conference on Information Technology in Construction.* Dresden, Germany: CIB Publication 304.

Schindler, M., & Eppler, M. (2003). Harvesting project knowledge: a review of projectlearning methods and success factors. *International Journal of Project Management, 21* (3), 219–228.

Sterman, J. (1992). Systems dynamics modelling for project management. Retrieved June 25, 2007, from web.mit.edu/jsterman/www/SDG/project.pdf

Sun, B., Xu, L., Pei, X., & Li, H. (2003). Scenario-based knowledge representation in case-based reasoning systems. *Expert Systems, 20* (2), 92–99.

Venkatraman, N. (1993). Continuous strategic alignment: exploiting information technology capabilities for competitive success. *European Management Journal, 11* (2), 139–149.

von Zedtwitz, M. (2002). Organizational learning through post-project reviews in R&D. *R&D Management, 32* (3), 255–268.

Watson, I. (2001). Knowledge management and case-based reasoning: a perfect match? In *Proc. of the Fourteenth Annual Conference of the International Florida Artificial Intelligence Research Society* (pp. 118–122). Menlo Park, CA: AAAI Press.

Weerd, I. (2006). Meta-modeling technique. Draft for the course method engineering 05/06.

Weggeman, M. (2004). The knowledge management model by M. Weggeman. Retrieved December 12, 2007, from www.irc.nl/content/download/9013/136183/file/20040101-The-KM-model.pdf.

Williams, T. (2003). Learning from projects. *Journal of Operational Research Society, 54,* 443–451.

Williams, T. (2004). Identifying the hard lessons from projects easily. *International Journal of Project Management, 22* (4), 273–279.

Yin, R. (2003). *Case Study Research: Design and Methods.* Thousand Oaks, CA: Sage Publications.

Index